Stanford House Staff Auxiliary

Guidebook
to
the
Bay
Area

A Guide for
Finding Your Way
Around the Bay
From Napa
to Monterey

By
Sheila K. Robinson

Napa Sonoma Press • Palo Alto • California

Published by:

Napa Sonoma Press
Post Office Box 1133
Palo Alto, CA 94301

Library of Congress Card Catalog Number 93-86355

International Standard Book Number 0-9637673-3-X

Softcover $9.95

Cover Design and Map Illustrations by Deborah Baldwin

Disclaimer

The purpose of this book is to provide accurate and complete information with the best effort having been made to make this possible. The information in this publication is not intended to recommend or dissaprove. Although the information contained herein has been compiled from sources deemed reliable, it is not guaranteed. The information is offered without recourse to the publisher and author. Napa Sonoma Press and the author disclaim all responsibility and liability to any person or entity with respect to any direct, consequential or incidental loss or damage caused or alleged to be caused by the information contained in this book. The information in this book is subject to change without notice.

TABLE of CONTENTS

CHAPTER ONE: Where to Shop

**CHAPTER TWO: Where to Bring
the Kids**

CHAPTER THREE: Stanford

CHAPTER FOUR: Annual Events

CHAPTER FIVE: Parks / Recreation

**CHAPTER SIX:
State and National Parks**

Foreword

I am delighted to have this opportunity to welcome you to Stanford University Hospital. The residency years are demanding and often filled with stress. At the same time they can be tremendously rewarding.

The House Staff Auxiliary provides a warm network of friends. They provide opportunities to explore the area and share experiences.

Please remember that the office of House Staff Administration is also available to the house staff as a resource. Our hours are 8 a.m. to 5 p.m. The telephone number is 723-5948.

Ann Dohn
Director,
House Staff Administration

Acknowledgments

It has been a rewarding experience to write this book and plan its development. The research, writing and editing necessary to produce this book was made possible by the Stanford House Staff Auxiliary.

Helen Bing, wife of Peter Bing and long time Stanford affiliate deserves special recognition. Her understanding and commitment to the housestaff members and their families is a valued asset. Her generosity provides the house staff with many social events in which the company of other intern/resident spouses is enjoyed. Helen Bing's support for the house staff has been an inspiration for writing this guidebook.

Ann Dohn, House Staff Officer Director, deserves special recognition for her input, concerns, and insights. Her guidance is extensive and has been significant to the development of this project.

Special thanks goes to K. Ashley Mooser, former editor of the *Enjoy Catalog* from the Palo Alto Recreation Department for permission to reprint the recreation listings.

Introduction

Welcome to Stanford. This book is designed to help you find your way around the Bay Area. Some of you reading this book are entering your medical residency at Stanford while others may be relocating to this area for maybe a Silicon Valley job transfer. If you're an incoming medical resident you've probably just learned of your "match" in the spring and beginning in a new community in June or early July gives you very little time to adjust. Actually, this book is designed to expedite your adjustment to this area whether or not you are associated with Stanford.

You might find it helpful to know where the major shopping centers are, where the parks are and what there is to do while you're in this beautiful Stanford area.

The idea for this book was born out of the Stanford House Staff Auxiliary which is a support group for wives and significant others of Stanford residents.

As this book introduces you to many different aspects of the Bay Area and many different places to go, some comments on safety are important. General safety tips on crime and natural danger should help you be aware of your environment as you visit an area previously unknown to you.

Unfortunately, the Bay Area as with most large urban areas is not free from violent crime, in fact, even the popular tourist spots such as Fisherman's Wharf in San Francisco has been subject to violent crimes. In the summer season San Francisco Police Department will step up its police patrol in tourist areas to help assure protection. Unfortunately, the wilderness areas can also be targeted crime areas.

The two most common tips often given by city policemen to protect yourself from falling victim to a violent crime are; 1) know your surroundings and 2) be alert about your surroundings. Travelling with a friend or in a group is also advised as a protective measure.

Swim and beach safety are two issues of concern for the beach goer as well as the lake swimmer. The Golden Gate National Recreation Association (415) 556-2236, provides a brochure containing such safety advice. Some of the essential safety tips for beach goers are: 1) stay on established trails along the coastal cliffs, 2) swim only at lifeguarded beaches and 3) swimmers, before entering the water, check for rip and longshore currents.

Fire safety tips for hikers include: 1) never smoke on hiking trails and 2) make fires only in allowed designated places provided by the park services.

Hikers can avoid the risk of getting lost when darkness falls by simply planning their return to the trailhead well in advance of sunset. Hikers also need to be aware of the Western Black-Legged tick. This tick although it is uncommon has been known to carry Lyme disease. The most common advice effective against a tick bite is to wear long pants and tuck the pant legs into your socks.

Earthquake preparedness has been given great attention in light of the October 17th earthquake of 1989. A special survival bag should be packed with items such as food for three to five days, medical supplies, extra flashlights, water and batteries. Many precautions can be done in and around the home for your protection in the event of a major earthquake. The American Red Cross and the Bay Area Regional Earthquake Preparedness Project can provide you with vital information.

The San Francisco Bay Area encompasses some of California's greatest parks, one of the world's favorite cities, and the college town of Palo Alto marking the end of the San Francisco Peninsula. Stanford is only one hour south of San Francisco and only two hours north of the Monterey Peninsula. The following pages should help you find shopping areas, parks, restaurants and more.

1

Chapter One

Where to Shop

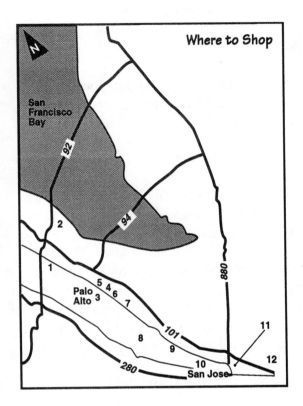

Chapter One

Where to Shop

1 Hillsdale Shopping Center
2 San Mateo Fashion Island
3 Stanford Shopping Center
4 Town & Country Village
5 Downtown Palo Alto
6 California Avenue District
7 San Antonio Shopping Center
8 Downtown Los Altos
9 Sunnyvale Town Center
10 Vallco Fashion Park
11 Valley Fair
12 Eastridge

Where to Shop

Palo Alto

Palo Alto offers many shopping locations to choose from. Five major areas to explore are mentioned here.

Downtown Palo Alto

Sometimes referred to as "The Village" downtown Palo Alto is located on University Avenue between Alma and Webster including the side streets between Lytton and Forest. There are many specialty shops, banks, galleries, cafes and restaurants. During the lunch hour and in the evenings, parking can be difficult. You can find underground public parking below city hall and on Ramona Street.

California Avenue District in Palo Alto

Just south of the Stanford campus California Avenue and El Camino intersect. 100 different shops including clothing stores, a pet shop, a comic book store, florist, donut shop, Printer's Inc. Bookstore and Mollie Stone's fine grocery store.

Midtown Palo Alto

Midtown is located south of Page Mill Road on Middlefield. The main intersection is Colorado and Middlefield. Here, you'll find three grocery stores, Midtown Market, the Co-op Market and Safeway. Peninsula Hardware and other specialty shops are in this area as well.

Stanford Shopping Center

Sand Hill Road, El Camino and Quarry Road border this beautifully landscaped outdoor mall. In the summer you can catch an evening Jazz concert in the Stanford Plaza. Nordstroms, Macy's, Neiman Marcus, I. Magnin are some of the department stores in the mall. There are many restaurants and specialty shops to choose from as well. You'll also find the Monterey Market which sells fresh produce at very reasonable prices. Directories are available throughout the mall. (415) 328-0600.

Town and Country Village

This shopping area is located just across from the Stanford campus on the corner of El Camino and Embarcadero. There are many specialty shops and restaurants to choose from as well as John's Market, a fine grocery store with a bakery/deli. Store front parking is available. (415) 325-3266.

13

South of Palo Alto

Downtown Los Altos

South of the Stanford campus on the Foothill Expressway is 1st Street of Los Altos. Los Altos has plenty of art galleries, specialty stores,and restaurants including The Costume Bank on State Street where you can rent costumes and Adventure Toys and Teacher Supplies on Main Street, a unique resource center for children's educational supplies.

Mountain View

Downtown Mountain View-Castro Street

The center of Mountain View has been renovated and along Castro Street you'll find many specialty shops, banks and some sidewalk cafes.

San Antonio Shopping Center

Located on the corner of San Antonio and El Camino in Mountain View you'll find; Sears, Ross Dress For Less, New York Fabrics, Best, Mervyn's, Payless Drugs among other shops. Nearby is Long's Drugs, Safeway, Target and Cost Plus. (415) 941-3794

Sunnyvale

Sunnyvale Town Center

Bordered by Mathilda, Iowa and Washington and
Sunnyvale Avenue, you will find 120 stores
including Macy' s and Montgomery Ward.
(408) 245-6585.

Cupertino

Vallco Fashion Park

On the corner of North Wolfe Road and Stevens
Creek Boulevard in Cupertino. This two story
indoor mall houses about 170 stores including
Sears, Penny's, The Emporium, The Express
(three stores in one) and an indoor ice skating
rink. (408) 255-5660.

San Jose

Downtown San Jose runs along Market and
Santa Clara Streets. The Pavilion Shops is a two
level outdoor shopping center that offers many
specialty shops, restaurants and some popular
night club spots . (408) 286-2076.

Valley Fair Shopping Center

Located on the corner of Stevens Creek Blvd and
Winchester right off of Highway 880. There are
almost 200 stores in this two story indoor mall
including Nordstrom's, Macy's and The Emporium. (408) 248-4451.

Eastridge Mall

Located on the corner of Tully Road and Capitol Expressway. There are about 140 stores including Sears, Penny's, and The Emporium. This is an indoor two story shopping mall. (408) 274-0360.

North of Palo Alto

San Mateo

Hillsdale Shopping Center

On the corner of Hillsdale Blvd and El Camino right off of Highway 101 and across the street is the Cal Train Station so you could even take the train to this shopping center. This is a two story indoor mall with about 150 stores including Emporium, Macys, Mervyn's, Nordstroms, Cost Plus and Sears. (415) 341-8095.

San Mateo Fashion Island

Located on the corner of Mariner's Island and Fashion Island Blvds. in San Mateo. This is an indoor mall with about 60 stores including Pier I Imports and Montgomery Ward and even an indoor ice skating rink. Take Foster City Bld. exit from 92 East. Turn left and then left again at the stoplight. (415) 570-5300.

Where the Bargains Are

Costco Discount warehouse with food, household and office supply items. Shopping here requires membership. Costco membership good at Price Club.

1000 N. Rengstorff, Mtn. View (415) 988-9766
40580 Albrae Street, Fremont (510) 683-6707
1600 Coleman Ave.Santa Clara (408) 988-8503

Price Club Membership shopping. Great for bulk buying. Good for stocking up on cleaning supplies, office supplies as well as many food items. Price Club membership good at Costco.

2300 Middlefield Road, Redwood City
(415) 369-3321.
150 Lawrence Station Road, Sunnyvale
(408) 730-1575.

Home Express This store carries a large variety of brand name items for the home like kitchen appliances made by Cuisinart and Braun. You'll also find ready to assemble furniture, housewares and electronics. Some discounts may be up to 60% off the regular retail price.

Westgate Mall on Prospect and Campbell in
San Jose (408) 374-2266
39125 Fremont Hub in Fremont (510) 795-7111

Frys Electronics Discount electronics store with a wide selection.
 360 Portage Avenue Palo Alto (415) 496-6000.
1177 Kern Avenue in Sunnyvale (408) 733-1770.

Chapter One

Where the Bargains Are

17

Whole Earth Access Store   Whole Earth sells general merchandise including housewares, electronics (VCR's, computers, TV's), books, cameras, major appliances, linens, family apparel, all with brand names and discounted prices.

401 Bayshore Blvd. San Francisco
(415) 285-5244
Fashion Island Mall in San Mateo
(415) 578-9200
3530 Stevens Creek Blvd. in San Jose
(408) 554 1500

K-Mart

Discount clothing, housewares, toys, sporting goods, garden tools, cosmetics, videos, small appliances, etc.

1155 Veterans, Redwood City (415) 364-7640.
1700 S. Delaware, San Mateo (415) 571-6177
975 S. Saratoga, Sunnyvale (408) 253-6350
3700 El Camino, Santa Clara (408) 247-2400

Target

Clothing and shoes for the family, toys, housewares, gardening supplies, small appliances, some furniture, video supplies, cosmetics, books. Often has sales.

555 Showers Dr., Mountain View (415)965-7644.
2485 El Camino, Redwood City (415)363-8940.
20745 Stevens Creek.,Cupertino (408) 725 2651.

Payless Drug Store

Seasonal items, cosmetics, toys, housewares, small appliances, shoes, cameras, plants, etc.

625 El Camino Real, Menlo Park (415) 326-2701
1040 Grant Road, Mountain View,(415) 968-9401
1165 El Camino, Sunnyvale (408) 732-0677.
10455 S De Anza, Cupertino (408) 966-2500.

Longs Drug Store

Seasonal items, camera-film department, greeting cards, gift items, cosmetics, pharmacy, some food items, school supplies, etc.

352 University Ave., Palo Alto (415)324-1667
1301 Broadway, Redwood City (415) 364-1113.
2630 El Camino, Mountain View (415)941-8650.
576 El Camino, Sunnyvale (408)739-4033.

Walgreen Drug Stores

Discount store with seasonal items, pharmacy, film developing, cosmetics, school supplies, greeting cards, cleaning supplies, etc.

300 University Ave., Palo Alto (415)322-7753.
121 El Camino, Mountain View (415) 961-7558.

Bargain Clothes

Ross Dress For Less

Clothing store with discount prices. Carries men's women's, children's clothes and accessories. You can also find tennis shoes at a bargain price. On sale you can find many seasonal items. New location on University Avenue in Palo Alto.

San Antonio Shopping Center. On the corner of El Camino and San Antonio Road in Mountain View. (415) 949-4060.
150 Woodside Plaza Shopping Center. On the corner of Woodside Road and Massachusetts Street in Redwood City. (415) 364-5990.
119 E. El Camino Real in Sunnyvale.
(408) 730- 4737.

Marshall's Department Store

Marshalls carries name brand clothes at discount prices. Clothes for children, men and women. Carries brand name shoes for children at reduced prices. When Marshall's marks down their prices, you're really getting a bargain.

1040 Grant Rd Mountain View, (415)965-4091
2525 El Camino, Redwood City (415) 366-1142
5777 Mowry Newark, (510)790 2556
5160 Stevens Creek, San Jose (408) 244 8962
2845 Meridian Ave., San Jose (408) 267 0922
4950 Almaden Expressway, San Jose
(408) 723 7677

T. J. Maxx

Many brand names offered at a discount. Clothes, women's shoes, men's and children's tennis shoes, and accessories for the family.

240 Walnut St., Redwood City (415) 365-2195.
1850 S. Grant St., San Mateo (415) 349-9544.
1825 Hillsdale, San Jose (408) 266-1110.
634 Blossom Hill, San Jose (408) 229-8062.

Dress Barn

For women's activewear, career clothing and accessories you'll find popular name brands at discount prices. The specials can offer up to a 50% discount.

700 El Camino in Menlo Park, (415) 328-2871.
1670 S. Bascom Avenue in Campbell
(408) 377-7544.

Pacific West Outlet Center

This outlet center houses more than twenty stores including a factory outlet for Levi Strauss, Liz Claiborne, Nike, Van Heusen, and Anne Klein. Located south of San Jose off highway 101 taking the Leavesley Road exit in Gilroy.
(408) 847-4155.

Resale Shops

The Goodwill Store

There are six fine locations to serve you from Palo Alto to San Jose. From blue jeans to costumes and furniture, it's worth checking out.

4085 El Camino Way, Palo Alto (415)494-1416.
855 El Camino, Mt. View (415) 969-3382.
2800 El Camino, Santa Clara (408) 247-2800.
151 E. Washington, Sunnyvale (408)736-8558.
1579 Meridian Ave., San Jose (408) 266-7151.
1125 Saratoga-Sunnyvale Cupertino
(408) 252-3193

The Kid's Clothesline

Resale shop with name brand clothes sizes 0 -14. You'll also find toys, shoes and some equipment.

10191 South DeAnza Blvd. in Cupertino. (near Stevens Creek Blvd.) (408) 865-0292.

Buttons and Bows

A children's boutique with new and pre-owned clothing. Large selection at very affordable prices. Play room in store. 6055-K Meridian Avenue in San Jose (408) 927-6614.

Bibbidy Bobbidy Boo-Tique

This re-sale shop carries sizes newborn to size six. You'll also find toys, books, and shoes. Located near 42nd and El Camino in San Mateo.

4222 Olympic Avenue. (4415) 341-6577.

American Cancer Society Discovery Shop

Located in downtown Menlo Park on Santa Cruz. Wide variety of clothes from children to adults.

746 Santa Cruz Avenue in Menlo Park
(415) 325-8939.

Treasure Box

Located right downtown on Castro Street in Mountain View. Carries children's, men and women's clothes.

453 Castro Street in Mountain View.
(415) 988-9768.

Turnabout Shop

This store carries fine clothing. You can find women's shoes, suits, children's clothes. Located right on El Camino just near the north corner of El Camino and California Street.

2335 El Camino Real in Palo Alto.
(415) 321-9853.

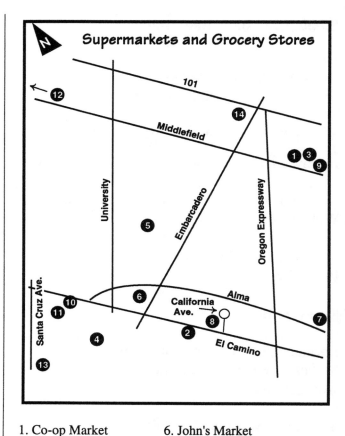

Supermarkets and Grocery Stores

1. Co-op Market
2. J J & F Foods
3. Midtown Market
4. Montery Market
5. Whole Foods Market

6. John's Market
7. Lucky's
8. Mollie Stone's Market
9. Safeway

10. Safeway
11. Trader Joe's
12. Sigona's Market

13. Draeger's

14. Lucky's

15. Safeway

*Los Altos locations not shown.

Supermarkets and Grocery Stores

Palo Alto   Palo Alto has a wide variety of markets. John's Market has a great take out deli and JJ & F Foods has wonderful fresh seafood. Mollie Stone's offers a large selection of organically grown fruits and vegetables as well as 100 item salad bar. Monterey Market has a wide selection of fresh fruit and vegetables at pretty good prices too. In addition to fresh fruits and vegetables, Whole Foods Market has a bakery and deli.

Co-op Market on Middlefield in Midtown
John's Market in Town & Country Village
J J & F Foods on College in Calif. Dist
Lucky's Supermarket on Alma
Lucky's on Embarcadero
Midtown Market on Middlefield in Midtown
Mollie Stone's Market in California Ave. District
Monterey Market in Stanford Shopping Center
Safeway Market on Middlefield in Midtown
Whole Foods Market on Emerson downtown

Menlo Park   Draeger's Supermarket is worth the trip just to see what a beautiful store it is. The first level has a magnificent bakery where you can buy fresh bread and fresh pastries. Upstairs you can watch the bakers at work and enjoy some of the deli selections in a cafeteria style setting.

Safeway on El Camino north of Stanford Center
Draeger's Supermarket on University
Trader Joe's on Menlo Avenue

Chapter One

Super markets and Grocery Stores

25

Redwood City   Sigona's Market offers great fresh produce and often runs special bargains.

Lucky's Supermarket in Woodside Plaza
Safeway on Woodside Road
Sigona's Farmers Market on Middlefield

Mountain View   Lucky's and Safeway at these locations are both large and very clean stores with wide shopping isles.

Lucky's on Rengstorff.
Safeway on California across from Best

Los Altos   You'll find another great Draeger's market here in Los Altos.   The Safeway is conveniently located right off the Foothill Expressway on 1st Street.   De Martini's Orchard sells organically grown vegetables and fruits.

Draeger's Supermarket on 1st Street
Lucky's on Grand Road
Safeway on 1st Street
Safeway on Homestead
De Martini's Orchard on San Antonio

Farmer's Markets

The following outdoor markets provide farm fresh produce including seasonal fruits, vegetables, dried fruits, eggs and plants and cut flowers. Some locations sell fish and seafood. Many local residents bring their own basket and come early.

Palo Alto   This busy outdoor market is held May through November every Saturday morning in the main Post Office parking lot on Gilman Street. Bargain flowers.

Los Altos   Located in the Bank of America parking lot on Fremont Avenue and Miramonte Street. Held mid-May through mid-November on Saturday mornings.

Menlo Park   Located between Menlo and Santa Cruz Street in downtown Menlo Park on Sundays 10:00am to 2:00pm.

Redwood City   Located in the City Parking Lot on Winslow Street south of Broadway. Held mid-May through early November.

San Jose   Located in Japantown on Jackson and 8th Streets. Held year-round on Sunday mornings.

Chapter One

Farmer's Markets

Shopping For Toys

Adventure Toys and Teacher's Supplies

Two story toy store with the second story housing many educational workbooks. On occasion Adventure Toys will host a play day where children are invited to come in and play with a select group of toys. 173 Main Street in Los Altos (415) 941-6043.

Chapter One

Toy Stores

Country Toy Store

Large toy store with a wide variety of toys for all ages of children. In Town & Country Village on corner of Embarcadero and El Camino in Palo Alto. (415) 327 6381.

Imaginarium

Two story children's toy store with a very creative selection of toys to choose from. Many educational toys. 101 Stanford Shopping Center in Palo Alto. (415) 321-4152

Palo Alto Sport Shop & Toy World

Wide selection of toys. Also carries sporting shoes, roller blades, and athletic wear. 526 Waverly in Palo Alto (415) 328-8555.

Earth Art and Frank's Scientific

A specialty store filled with nature and science items for children and hobbiests. 470 Hamilton in Palo Alto (415) 324-0834.

San Antonio Hobby Shop

This store carries a large selection of model trains, airplanes wood ship models, cars, and other model kits. It is located in the San Antonio Shopping Center in Mountain View. 2550 El Camino Real in Mountain View (415) 941-1278.

Toys R' Us

This nationwide chain toy store has everything from party supplies to bicycles for children. This is a warehouse full of children's items.

Peninsula Boardwalk Shopping Center
202 Walnut Redwood City (415) 367-0186
Saratoga-Sunnyvale Road and El Camino
in Sunnyvale (408) 732-00331.

Talbot's Cyclery, Talbot's Hobbies, and Talbot's Toyland

Huge store with a baby furniture section, a hobby section with trains, video games, a bicycle section and a huge selection of toys. 445 South B Street in San Mateo (415) 342-0126.

Hearth Song

This is a toy store filled with traditional toys made from natural fabrics, wood and ceramics.

1812 4th Street, Berkeley (510) 849-3956
1344 Burlingame Ave, Burlingame
(415)-579-5711

FAO Schwarz Toy Store

Located at 48 Stockton Street on the corner of O'Farrell Street. (415) 394-8700. This is a three story toy store that has toys ranging from $1 to $15,000.00. The mechanical clock tower and the soldier make for a very impressive entry.

The Wooden Horse

This toy store carries toys from around the world. Located in Los Gatos in Kings Court Center. 798 Blossom Hill Road, (408) 356-8821.

Toy Liquidators/Toys Unlimited

Prices in this toy store can be as much as 70% off the regular retail price. This company buys the surplus close-out inventory from manufacturers like Hasbro, Playskool and Fisher Price. Mark down specials are practically a give-away. 899 Howard in San Francisco (415) 243-8518 and another location at the Pacific West Outlet Center in Gilroy (408).

Shopping for Infant's Clothes

Lullaby Lane

This store carries clothes for infants and toddlers. Girl's sizes go up to 6x. Lullaby Lane also carries baby furniture. 556 San Mateo Avenue in. San Bruno (415) 588-7644.

Baby Super Discount

Carries clothes in sizes infants to 24 months. Also carries baby furniture. 522 S. Bascom in San Jose (408) 293-0358.

Bellini

This store carries Italian baby furniture as well as baby accessories and gifts. Offers a nice infant clothes section. 1145 El Camino in Menlo Park (415) 329-8488. 2003 Camden in San Jose (408) 559-7676.

Chapter One

Infant's Clothes

Bookstores

Chapter One

Book- stores

Printer's Inc.   Coffeeshop within bookstore. Maintains an interesting author event schedule. 310 California Ave. Palo Alto (415) 327-6500. 301 Castro St. Mountain View (415) 468-2198.

Kepler's Books and Magazines   Kepler's offers a busy author event schedule and probably the largest selection of titles in the Bay Area. Indoor - outdoor cafe right next door. 1010 El Camino Real in Menlo Park (415) 324-4321.

Stanford Book Store   Lasuen (on campus near Tressider Union). This tri-level book store carries a wide selection of books as well as Stanford clothing items, computers, software, CD's and a sweet shop. 329-1217.

Stacey's Bookstore   This bookstore has several locations and offers books on hundreds of sub- jects. 219 University Avenue in Palo Alto, (415) 326-0681. In San Francisco at 581 Market Street (415) 421-4687 and at 383 Sacramento Street (415) 397-7935. 19625 Steven's Creek Blvd. in Cupertino (408) 253-7521.

Thunderbird   Located just south of the Monterey Penninsula in the Barnyard off of highway 1 in Carmel. This bookstore has the Central Coast's largest selection. You can enjoy your book over lunch, dinner, or coffee and dessert. Monthly events. (408) 624-1803

Children's Bookstores

Kepler's Books and Magazines

Kepler's Kids is an author event program especially for children with special readings, signings and children's activites. Large selection of children's books. 1010 El Camino Real in Menlo Park (415) 324-4321.

The Linden Tree

Large store with a large selection of children's books and records. Many visiting authors, readings, signing events. 170 State Street in Los Altos (415) 949-3390.

Hicklebee's

Huge store with large children's selection. 1378 Lincoln Avenue, San Jose (408) 292-8880. 280 to San Jose to Bird Ave. Right to Willow, to Lincoln. Just before Minnesota Ave. on the left.

Chanticleer

A very special selection of children's books. Located in historical downtown Los Gatos. 23 East Main St., Los Gatos (408) 354-3331.

Chapter One

Children's Bookstores

Video Rental Stores

Blockbuster Video   Blockbuster rents videos at a two-day minimum rate for just under $4.00. Large selection and very up to date on the new releases. You pay when you check out the videos. Has a large video game rental selection.

102 University Ave., Palo Alto (415) 328-7852.
4102 El Camino, Palo Alto (415) 424-1362.
1365 El Camino, Menlo Park (415) 326-4797.
2505 El Camino, Redwood City (415)361-8233.
1040 Grant Rd, Mountain View (415)962-9500.
444 El Camino, Sunnyvale (408) 720-0445

The Wherehouse   Great single day video rental prices for just under $2.00. Up to date on new releases. You pay when you return the videos.

700 El Camino, Menlo Park (415) 322-0156.
1932 El Camino, Redwood CIty (415) 364-2474.
1939 El Camino, Mountain View (415) 961-3268.
563 El Camino, Sunnyvale (408) 733-0644.
1060 El Camino, Sunnyvale (408) 247-7433.

Videoscope   This store is well organized and has many hard to find titles in addition to the popular titles. Reasonable rental rates.

3731 El Camino, Palo Alto (415) 493-0500

Chapter One

Video Stores

Music Stores

Gryphon Stringed Instruments A music store for the guitar lover. A wide selection of instructional books, a sound room and a classroom for group instruction.
211 Lambert Avenue in Palo Alto. 493-2131

Melody Lane If you're looking for sheet music, please inquire in this store. Located in downtown Palo Alto on Ramona. Can also enter from the parking lot next to Lytton Plaza.
532 Ramona. (415) 323-5791.

Swain's House of Music Located in downtown Palo Alto on the corner of University and Kipling. Family owned and operated. Music instruction and instrument rental.
451 University Avenue. (415) 324-1635.

Tower Records Large selection of albums and CD singles. Large classical selection.
630 San Antonio Road in Mountain View.
(415) 941-7900.

Wollmer's Well supplied store and offers a great instrument rental program for school programs in that your rental fees apply to the purchase of the instrument. Located in San Mateo on the corner of 4th and S. B Streets.
225 E. 4th Avenue. (415)343-2788.

Chapter One

Music Stores

Bike Shops

Here are some of the shops in the immediate Stanford area. More listed in the appendix.

Palo Alto Bicycles   This bike shop carries a wide variety of specialty bicycles and bike accessories. Also offers a service department. Store is more than 50 years old. 171 University Avenue, Palo Alto 328-7411. Service Dept. 328-7419.

Chapter One

Bike Shops

The Bike Connection   This is a great family bike shop and carries used bikes too. Also has a rental and a repair shop. Two locations:

Campus Bike Shop   Located right on the Stanford campus for more than 40 years. Also offers repair and rental services and also sells used bikes. 551 Salvatierra. (415) 325-2945.

Recyclery   Located right across the street from the southeast end of the Stanford campus on El Camino. Sells new and used bikes and has a large repair shop. 1955 El Camino Palo Alto (415) 328-8900.

Wheelsmith   Located on the corner of Hamilton and Emerson right across from the Creamery in Palo Alto. A huge store with a complete repair shop downstairs. Upstairs you can watch videos of bike races, read bike magazines or shop for bike accessories or bikes. Run by John and Ric Hjirberg who started their bike shop from their garage more than fifteen years ago. (415)324-0510.

2

Chapter Two

Where to Bring The Kids

Local Fun

Palo Alto Jr. Museum

This children's museum features many hands on exhibits, workshops, and animal demonstrations. Exhibits are very well planned for an interactive museum experience. Children can interact with the displays as well as observe very interesting exhibits. This children's museum is one of the oldest children's museums in the country. In addition to exhibits, the museum offers special children's programs, planetarium shows, slide shows and classes. 1451 Middlefield Road, between Lucy Stern Center and Rinconada Park) (415) 329-2111.

Palo Alto Children's Zoo

This small children's zoo is located adjacent to the children's museum. Children can watch the birds and turtles in the pond and see a fox, raccoons and an owl. Reptiles can be observed through glass cages. The interpretive program introduces some of the local wildlife to the public via question and answers sessions. Programs are available by reservation. (415) 329-2610 for more information. The zoo also offers animal get acquainted lectures on Saturdays at 11:15 and 3:00 pm and on Sundays at 2:30pm. (415) 329-2111.

Palo Alto Children's Theatre

Located in Lucie Stern Center at 1305 Middlefield
Road, Palo Alto. This theatre provides performances given by child actors ages 8 through 18.
In the summer there is a special Summertime Hot
Dog Theatre with performances given outside on
the stage next to the Secret Garden. Hot dogs,
drinks, chips and ice cream are sold at very
reasonable prices. Advance ticket purchase
strongly encouraged as these productions often
sell out early. Season tickets are available.
Picnics are welcome. (415) 329-2216

Barbie Doll Hall of Fame

460 Waverly Street at University Avenue in Palo
Alto. The world's largest collection of Barbie
dolls is located in this special museum. The
collected outfits also reflect America's fashions
trends over the past thirty years (415) 326-5841.

Palo Alto Cultural Center

In addition to featuring exhibits of a variety of
fine arts, the center offers performing arts and
dance productions for children. The Palo Alto
Youth Symphony offers performances throughout
the year. Special weekend art workshops are
offered and adult art classes are offered including
classes in drawing, painting and ceramics. Located at 1313 Newell on the corner of
Embarcadero and Newell and right next to the
main library. (415) 329-2366.

**Chapter
Two**

**Local
Fun**

Museum of American Heritage

Come and see a business office of the 1920's, and a kitchen, and grocery store of the 1930's time of the Great Depression. Other exhibits change four times a year and reflect the early 1900's. Located at 275 Alma Street in Palo Alto near the Menlo Park border. (415) 3221-1004

The Stanford Theatre

This theater shows films made before the 1960's and often features film festivals. The 1920's Wurlitzer organ is a delightful addition to the fun filled silent movies shown in this beautifully renovated theater. Located at 221 University Ave. Five and under require special arrangements for evening showings. (415) 324-3700.

NASA/Ames Research Center

This research center is a field lab for space technology and aeronautics. Tours are offered through a flight simulator and a wind tunnel. Advance reservations required for this two mile tour. Ages 9 and up. Take highway 101 to the Moffett Blvd exit in Mountain View. (415) 604-6497.

Sunset Magazine

Located in Menlo Park on the corner of Willow and Middlefield. Tours of garden showing native plants of the west, the test kitchen and the editorial building are given daily. This activity is more for adults. Allow one hour. (415) 321-3600.

The Allied Arts Guild

Located at the end of Cambridge Avenue on Arbor Road in Menlo Park. An Old World atmosphere where a glass-blower, candlemaker, weaver and other craftsmen practice their crafts. The courtyards are surrounded by Spanish style buildings and beautiful gardens. There's also a restaurant. (415) 329-3259.

Woodside Store

Built by a pioneer in 1854 this store used to serve as a post office, a dentist's office and a library and was the first store established between San Francisco and San Jose located in Woodside. The store is now a museum and you can see antique machinery such as an apple press. Open Tuesday, Thusday and weekends. (415) 851-7615.

Filoli House and Garden

As seen on the television show *Dynasty*, this mansion is available for guided two-hour tours. The mansion is surrounded by 16 acres of wonderfully landscaped gardens. Tour reservations required. Ages 12 and up. Tours are available mid-February through mid-November. The Nature Program is for all ages and includes a nature hike. Fees. Located one mile north of Edgewood on Canada Road off of highway 280 in Woodside. 364-2880.

41

Foothill College Radio Electronics Museum

This museum displays old radios and other robotic exhibits. The museum in located on the Foothill College campus. Admission . (415) 949-7383.

Foothill College Observatory

Also located on the Foothill College campus is the observatory. Star watching and other programs are available. (415) 949 1431.

Rancho San Antonio

This park is very popular as it offers meadows, trails, Deer Hallow Farm, bike paths, etc. Take highway 280 to Foothill Expressway to Cristo Rey Drive. Deer Hallow Farm (415) 966-6331.

Hidden Villa Ranch

Located in Los Altos Hills, the Hidden Villa Ranch is well known for its educational programs. Farm tours and summer camps are available. From 280 take the Moody Road exit, then right to 26870 Moody Road (415) 948-4690.

East Bay

Ardenwood Historic Farm

This historical farm offers a look at the way a farm was in the late 1800's. There are tours, farm animals, wagon rides and a blacksmith's shop. Admission. Go over the Dumbarton Bridge and take highway 84 to Ardenwood Boulevard in Fremont. (510) 796-0199

Children's Fairyland

This park is said to have been the inspiration for Disneyland and is located in Lakeside Park, on the eastern edge of Lake Merritt. Children's Fairyland is a child sized amusement park featuring many fairy tales. (510) 832-3609.

Oakland Zoo

Located in Knowland Park. The zoo also has a petting zoo, rides including a carousel and picnic facilities. Located off of Highway 580 on the Golf Links Road exit. 510-632-9525.

Lawrence Hall of Science

Located on the U.C. Berkeley campus, this science hall has many interesting exhibits, one of which is the Dinosaur Exhibit which features robotic replicas. (510) 642-5132 (taped message).

Bay Area Discovery Museum

Located near the Golden Gate Bridge at 555 East Fort Baker Road, Sausalito. The museum is spacious and offers many hands-on activities. There's the Space Maze, the Underwater Adventure Tunnel, a Discovery Theatre where the children can put on make up and perform on stage! Check for special children's workshops too. For directions and further information: (415) 332-7644 or 332-9646.

Jack London Square

On the waterfront of Oakland's Estuary, this marina area has a variety of seafood restaurants and art galleries. The shopping area overlooks the estuary along with Jack London's log cabin and the Heinhold's First and Last Chance Saloon. (510) 893-7956.

Marine World Africa USA

Located in Vallejo, allow for at least a 90 minute commute from the Stanford area. You can also ride the ferry boat from Pier 39. Marine World easily takes a full day to see all of the sights. In addition to a full day of live shows, the children can pet animals as trainers walk through the park with different animals. The water ski show is very exciting. The shark exhibit lets you walk through a large aquarium. (707) 644-4000.

San Jose Sights

Lick Observatory

At the top of Mt. Hamilton is this modern observatory. You can study the stars with very sophisticated telescope equipment. Star gazing is available in the summer. 408-274-5060.

Winchester Mystery House

This bizarre four story mansion has more than 150 rooms with many oddities designed and owned by the heir to the rifle fortune, Sara Winchester. Construction continued on this home for more than 35 years. Tours available. 408-247-2101. It is located off of highway 280 on Winchester Blvd.

Great America Amusement Theme Park

This is a huge amusement park divided into five areas. Many rides including the Vortex, a stand up roller coaster. Many stage shows, games and concerts. Located off of highway 101 on the Great America Parkway exit. (408) 408 988-1800.

Rosicrucian Egyptian Museum

On corner of Park and Naglee. Walk through a replica of a tomb. Many Egyptian artifacts and a mummy collection. The Rosicrucian Planetarium is located next door. Museum is for all ages. Planetarium is for ages 5 and up. 408-287-2807.

947- 36 36

9-5 daily
museum & planeto
6.75   4 -
3.50   3 -

Chapter Two

San Jose Sights

N
880/ALAMED
R NAGLEE
L PARK

45

Raging Waters Theme Park

This outdoor water park has more than thirty water attractions including river rides, wading pools, water slides, inner-tube rafting and a sandy beach. 408-270-8000.

Kelley Park/ Happy Hollow Park and Zoo

This park complex includes marionette shows, a petting zoo, picnic and play areas, a Japanese garden and the San Jose Historical Museum which features historical homes, businesses and shops from the late 1800's. Take Story Road exit off of 101 South, then left on Senter Road.

Happy Hollow	408-292-8188
Museum	408-287-2290
Japanese Garden	408-295-2708

Alum Rock Park- Youth Science Institute

This park offers over ten miles of trails including horse and bicycle trails. Located at the end of Alum Rock Avenue in San Jose. The Youth Science Institute offers science programs including the study of reptiles, plants, and insects. 408-258-4322.

Emma Prusch Farm Park

Although this farm has an urban location, here you can walk through a barn filled with farm animals including sheep and pigs and even a cow. In San Jose on S. King Road. 408-926-5555.

Children's Discovery Museum

This museum offers hands on exhibits where the children can walk through and experience their surroundings. Exhibits include a display of an ATM machine, postal process, city streets, and a special art exhibit where the children can create their own artwork. Located on Woz Way in downtown San Jose. 408-298-5437 or KIDS.

Tu-Sat 10-5
Sun Noon-5
6.00 adult
4.00 child
3-4 hrs

Tech Museum of Innovation

This museum used to be called The Garage and Technology Center of Silicon Valley named after the birth of the Silicon Valley via the modest Palo Alto garage used by Hewlett and Packard. The museum offers hands on exhibits which include the science areas of robotics, space, microelectronics. Special programs are available. Located across from the San Jose Convention Center in McCabe Hall. 408- 279-7150.

San Jose Museum of Art

Family Sunday encourages family participation and is free. Family Sunday is the first Sunday of each month. The activities are directed towards the elementary school aged child. Activities include musicians, storytellers, puppet shows and tours. Art classes for all ages are offered including classes in painting and drawing. Located at 110 S. Market in San Jose. (408) 294-2787.

Chapter Two

South of San Jose

Just South of San Jose

Saratoga

Saratoga and Los Gatos are neighboring towns and can be reached by taking highway 17 south towards Santa Cruz. Take the exit for Los Gatos via route 9. Route 9 and Big Basin Road is the main intersection for Saratoga. You will find many specialty boutiques, antique shops, cafes and restaurants. The town is very appealing and offers the charm of a small village.

Villa Montalvo Center for the Arts

A bird sanctuary and an arboretum are part of this center. Indoor and outdoor theater offers many performing arts events. Located in Saratoga on Montalvo Road. 408 741-3421.

Los Gatos

North Santa Cruz Avenue is the main street bordered on either side by many shops and restaurants including the Chart House, Pedro's, and the California Cafe. The Old Town area is located along University Avenue. The Old Town shopping area used to house Los Gatos High School. Los Gatos Creek offers more than six miles of trail hiking. Los Gatos suffered great damage in the 1989 earthquake. The city has set an example of how to rebuild and restore many of the historical buildings. The trail to the Lexington Reservoir can be reached from Main Street.

Santa Cruz

Downtown Santa Cruz was heavily damaged in the 1989 earthquake. Santa Cruz has been rebuilt and beautifully renovated since. Santa Cruz has many art galleries, museums, and restaurants all situated in this attractive seaside village. Steamer Lane is a popular surfing spot along West Cliff Drive.

Beach and Boardwalk   The boardwalk is an amusement park overlooking Santa Cruz beach and offers many games, and rides including the Giant Dipper roller coaster. The boardwalk also has an indoor amusement center offering some history exhibits and an assortment of games. The boardwalk is located on Beach Street in Santa Cruz. (408) 423-5590. On the wharf adjacent to the boardwalk, you'll find many seafood restaurants.

Roaring Camp and Big Trees Railroad is located in the Santa Cruz Mountains in Felton. Felton is about five miles north of Santa Cruz. Roaring Camp is a railroad station built to look like a logging camp from the 1800s when narrow-gauge railroads were part of the pioneer days of the West. The narrow-gauge steam engine trainride takes you through the redwood trees in the Santa Cruz mountains. The Santa Cruz, Big Trees & Pacific Railway Company offers a two and one half hour roundtrip trainride to the Santa Cruz Beach Boardwalk. (408) 225-4484.

Mystery Spot   Located in Santa Cruz on Branciforte Drive (Market Street becomes Branciforte Drive). The Mystery Spot offers tours of a portion of a redwood forest that appears to defy the law of gravity. Allow at least a half hour for the tour. (408) 423-8897.

Joseph Long Marine Laboratory   This research laboratory is affiliated with the University of California. There is a touch tank similar to a California tidepool, and a more than eighty foot long skeleton of a blue whale and an aquarium. Tours are available. Open Tuesday through Sunday 1-4pm. (408) 459-4308. The laboratory is located at the end of Delaware Avenue on Shaffer Road in Santa Cruz.

3

Chapter Three

Stanford

The Palo Alto Farm

Leland Stanford lived in San Francisco and decided that he wanted to buy a country home so his son, Leland Jr. could have more room to play outdoors. So in 1876 Leland Stanford purchased 650 acres of land which he named as the Palo Alto Farm and which later became Stanford University in 1891.

Guided Campus Tours

Tours are given daily at 11:00am and 3:15pm. The tour takes about 45 minutes and meets in front of the information booth at the main quadrangle entrance. To arrange for a guided tour of campus please call 723-2560.

Rodin Sculpture Garden

This garden displays the largest public collection in the world of bronze sculpture by Auguste Rodin. The sculptures are located adjacent to the Leland Stanford Jr. Museum of Art (which has been closed due to earthquake damage from the 1989 quake). Garden tours are held Wednesday, Saturday and Sunday at 2:00p.m. (415) 723-3469.

Stanford University Hospital and Lucile Salter Packard Children's Hospital at Stanford

The Stanford University Hospital and the Stanford University Clinics were completed in 1959 with an addition to the clinics completed in 1965 and an addition to the hospital completed in 1976. Lucile Salter Packard Children's Hospital at Stanford opened in June of 1991. It is a state of the art children's hospital. You can either enter on Welch Road or walk through Stanford University Hospital. For tour information call information at 723-4000 and 497-8044 for the Children's Hospital.

The Stanford Museum

Mrs. Leland Stanford had this museum built in memorial to her son who died an untimely death at the early age of sixteen. The acquisitions are all from private benefactions. The Committee for Art at Stanford holds an annual Treasure Mart to raise purchase money for the museum. The Treasure Mart is a sale of furniture, donated art items, jewelry, books, and many household items. The museum is located on Lomita Drive and Museum Way on Campus and is closed indefinitely due to heavy damage in the 1989 earthquake. The sculpture collection of sculptor Auguste Rodin is a highlight of this museum. The sculpture garden is open and tours are available weekends and Wednesdays at 2:00pm.
(415) 725-0462.

Thomas Welton Stanford Art Gallery

The art gallery is open and is housing some of the Stanford museum exhibits. Located on Serra Street across from the Business School near Hoover Tower. Open Tuesday through Friday, 10:00a.m. - 5:00p.m.; Weekends, 1:00p.m. - 5:00p.m. (415) 723-2842. The Nathan Cummings Art Building is next to this gallery and offers student exhibitions Tuesday through Friday 10:00am to 5:00pm and weekends 1:00 - 5:00pm (415) 723-2842.

Hoover Tower

Herbert Hoover sent material to Stanford during World War I which is now documented in the Hoover Institution on War. On the ground floor two rooms exhibit items from both President and Mrs. Hoover's lives. Near Serra Street and Galvez. You can take an elevator to the top of the tower to get a great view of the campus and surrounding area. Admission. (415) 723-1754 for tour information.

Stanford Linear Accelerator Center

The two-mile long linear accelerator won the Nobel Prize award in physics in 1976. The re-search involved within this accelerator is in elementary particle physics. Located at 2575 Sand Hill Road in Menlo Park. (415) 926-2204 Tours of the research laboratory are available by reservation.

Lively Arts at Stanford

The outdoor Frost Amphitheater, The Memorial Auditorium, the Dinkelspiel Auditorium and the Little Theater offer both theatrical and musical productions. The Lively Arts Calendar runs from October through April.

Music The music program offers a variety of performances including choral singers, brass quntets, string quartets, chamber music, folk music, and jazz quartets. To obtain a Lively Arts brochure, please call (415) 725-ARTS.

Recitals Many informal student recitals take place in Campbell Recital Hall. These concerts are free and open to the public. The Music Department Concert Line phone number is (415) 723-2720.

Summer Concerts at Stanford The Stanford Music Department sponsors many performances during the summer including performances by the Stanford Summer Symphony Chorus. There are also many recital opportunities. Tickets can be purchased at the Tressider Ticket Office (415) 723-4317. The Music office phone number is (415) 723-3811.

Theater and Dance The Lively Arts offers a variety of theatrical performances including children's theater, adult stand up improvisational comedy and musicals . Dance productions include modern, baroque and ballet.

55

Stanford House Staff Privileges

Sports   The facilities available to the housestaff and their families includes 26 tennis courts, riding stables and two swimming pools. Your spouse can take advantage of the many sports facilities by obtaining a spouse card. To obtain a spouse card, the spouse must bring the housestaff member's Stanford ID and another ID reflecting both of your names (for example, a bank statement or a checkbook) to the Athletic Office. The Athletic Office is located on Campus Drive and Galvez.

De Guerre Pool   features three outdoor pools and eight indoor handball/racquetball courts. Lap swimming is great in this pool. There is also an area roped off for families. Green grass is adjacent to the poolside.

Roble and Encina Gymnasiums house facilities for badminton, weight training and dance. Roble Pool is located adjacent to Roble Gym. (415) 723-1021.

Stanford Golf Course The golf course is open to Stanford faculty and staff with no special privileges for housestaff. The pro shop is located at the end of Campus Drive East.

Stanford Equestrian Center Located on Electioneer Road off of Campus Drive. The equestrian center is open to the public and offers English riding lessons and boarding. 322-5713.

Bing Exercise Room   Helen and Peter Bing donated this exercise room to the house staff so there could be an onsite place for the residents to exercise (not open for public use). Located on the 4th Floor On Call Quarters. This exercise room is complete with weight machines, exercise bikes and music. Individualized training for house staff is available.

Bing Dining Room   Located on the third floor of the hospital as you exit the escalator. This is a beautiful dining room generously donated by Peter and Helen Bing exclusively for Stanford housestaff. Meal cards are accepted here. Annual social events are also held here.

House Staff Library

Located on the fourth floor in the on-call quarters. This library has been generously donated by Helen and Peter Bing. Medline access and software are available through an Apple computer located in the library.

Stanford Libraries

With your house staff card or your spouse card you are eligible for library use privileges. The libraries include the Lane Medical Library, Green, Meyer and the Law Library.

4

Chapter Four

Annual Events

Annual Events

Summer / June

Brown Bag Concert Series   These series of freeweekly noon concerts are presented at Cogswell Plaza in Palo Alto.   Bring your own lunch. 329-2261.

Stanford Summer Series   Music, dance and theatre performances through August. Variety of Stanford locations. 723-2551.

Twilight Concerts in the Park   A series of free concerts through August located at different Palo Alto parks. 329-2261.

Union Street Spring Festival   Hundreds of artists and craftspeople display their work in booths along the Union Street in San Francisco. Outdoor cafes and entertainment are available.

Summer Reading Program Check your local library for summer events involving the summer reading program. Palo Alto libraries have "Wacky Wednesdays " for summer reader participants.

Sand Castle Celebration held in City Hall Plaza in Palo Alto. The outdoor patio is converted into giant sandboxes for this event. (415) 329-2493.

Chapter Four

Annual Events

July

Connoisseur's Marketplace   A street festival featuring gourmet food, wine, arts and crafts and entertainment. Located on Santa Cruz Avenue in Menlo Park. 325-2818

Menlo Park 4th of July Parade The Menlo Park Recreation Department organizes this event which is fun for the whole family. (415) 858-3470

Fireworks at Crissy Field in San Francisco. The evening of the 4th of July offers lots of entertainment and music and when it's dark, there's a terrific fireworks show. (415) 556-4460.

Los Altos Art and Wine Festival   Located on Main Street in Los Altos. A variety of food and craft booths are offered. (415) 949-5282.

TGIF Concert Series   This series runs through August and is held at City Hall in Palo Alto. (415) 329-2261.

Comedy Celebration   This event is located in Golden Gate Park in San Francisco. The entertainment is provided by local comedians. You may want to pack a picnic. (415) 543-3030.

August

Summer Carnival   The Palo Alto Recreation Department sponsors a "penny carnival" in Rinconada Park. Game booths, entertainment and plenty of prizes. (415) 329-2261.

Palo Alto Arts Celebration Held on University Avenue. Similar to the Los Altos Arts and Wine Festival. Many arts, crafts and food booths. Two day event. (415) 346-4446.

Autumn / September

Kings Mountain Art Fair Artists display their work in Woodside at Kings Mountain Community Center. 851-2710.

Mountain View Art and Wine Festival This is an annual event offering a variety of food booths and entertainment held on Castro Street in Mountain View. 968-8378.

FCL Harvest Festival This event offers children's activities along with a flea market, a book sale and plenty of arts and crafts, food booths and entertainment. Located at Hidden Villa in Los Altos Hills. 851-8182.

International Street Performers Festival This event is held on Pier 39 in San Francisco. The entertainment is provided by San Francisco's best street performers and other international performers. (415) 981-PIER.

October

Halloween Spooktacular This event held at Mitchell Park in Palo Alto offers storytelling and treats. (415) 329-2261.

Chapter Four

Events in Autumn

61

Halloween Window Display Contests You can find halloween window displays in Los Altos on Main and State Streets. For locations in Menlo Park and Palo Alto call 325-2818 and 329-2380.

Halloween Party Holbrook-Palmer Park in Atherton. Fun for the kids. (415) 688-6534.

Japanese Festival Mitchell Park in Palo Alto. A weekend event with many food booths.

Fleet Week Celebrating the Navy's birthday, the City of San Francisco invites the public to watch the Blue Angels (Navy's precision flight team) perform over San Francisco Bay. (415) 981-8030.

Half Moon Bay Art & Pumpkin Festival Craft booths, pumpkin carving and a variety of pumpkin foods are offered at this event. Half Moon Bay offers many colorful pumpkin patches during this time of year. Traffic can be very congested along 92 so start early. (415) 726-9652.

November

The Big Game Each year Cal and Stanford draw a huge cross town crowd for a highly spirited football game. 329-2261.

Festival of Lights Parade This annual parade is held on Main and State Streets in Los Altos. (415) 941-3378.

Teddy Bear Film Festival and Parade
This event is held on the weekend after Thanksgiving. Tickets should be purchased in advance. Children usually bring their teddy bears and march in an informal parade followed by a children's film. This event is held in the Pacific Film Archive located on the corner of Durant Avenue and College Avenue in Berkeley. (510) 642-1412.

Winter - December

Santa Claus Comes to Town   Each year Santa arrives on California Avenue and in Downtown Palo Alto. The children can greet him. 329-2261.

Santa Comes to the Menlo Park Train Station
This event features a parade. Held at the Menlo Park Train Station. 325-2818.

Pickle Family Circus   This circus has a 30 foot trapeze, a jazz band and assorted jugglers. Each year during the Christmas holidays, the Pickle Family Circus performs at the Palace of Fine Arts, 3601 Lyon Street in San Francisco (the Marina District near the Golden Gate Bridge). (415) 561-0360.

January

East-West Shrine Game   Another great football game. This one to benefit Shriners Hospitals. Held at Stanford University Stadium in Palo Alto .(415) 723-1021.

Chapter Four

Events in Winter

63

Kid's Triathlon Children ages 7-16 run bike and swim within their own age group. All athletes must wear helmets while biking and caps while swimming. Entry blanks available at Lucie Stern and Mitchell Park Centers. Event held at Rinconada Park in Palo Alto. (415) 329-2380.

Chinese New Year Celebration & Parade This celebration began in 1851 and features the Golden Dragon Parade. Sometimes this even falls on the calendar in February or March. It is held in Chinatown, San Francisco. (415) 391-2000.

San Francisco Zoo Run This is a family-oriented run covering about a three mile course through the zoo. The course includes the Primate Discovery Center and Penguin Island. (415) 753-7061.

Whale Watching From November through January more than 1000 gray whales will make the trip from the Bering Sea to the warmer waters of Baja California. The whales make the trip back in the spring during March and April. You can watch from shore from places like the Ano Nuevo State Reserve north of Santa Cruz, Point Reyes in Marin, and Point Lobos on the Monterey Peninsula.

Ano Nuevo Elephant Seal Tours From December through April you can take a guided tour with state park guides and learn about the elephant seals who come ashore to breed their young. It is amazing to see these huge mammals in their natural environment. (415) 879-0595.

Spring / April

Easter Egg Hunts
Burgess Field in Menlo Park (415) 858-3470.
Mitchell Park Bowl in Palo Alto (415) 329-2261.

Cherry Blossom Festival   Held at the Japan
Center area bounded by Geary, Laguna, Fillmore
and Post. A Japanese-style celebration with
dancing, a variety of Japanese ceremonies,
demonstrations and a colorful parade.
(415) 563-2313.

May

Black and White Ball   This annual black-tie
event is a benefit for the children's May Fete
Parade. Live music and gourmet food. Held in
six different locations in Palo Alto. 329-2380.

Day at the Park   A carnival with food booths
and entertainment held at Holbrook-Palmer Park
in Atherton (415) 688-6534.

May Fete Parade This parade is especially for
children. Held on University Avenue in Palo Alto
with a carnival following at the parade's end at
Addison Elementary School. The carnival offers
over twenty booths including food, prizes and a
variety of games. 329-2261.

Mayfest Weekend   A parade along with wine
tasting, arts and crafts, a flea market and a pan-
cake breakfast. Held on Main and State Streets in
Los Altos (415) 948-1455.

**Chapter
Four**

**Events
in
Spring**

5

Chapter Five

Parks
and Recreation

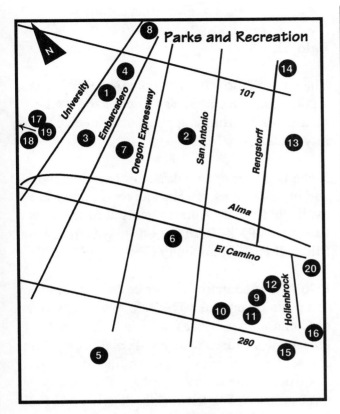

Parks and Recreation

1. Rinconada Park
2. Mitchell Park
3. Johnson Park
4. Pardee Park
5. Foothills Park
6. Briones Park
7. Peers Park
8. Baylands

9. Heritage Oaks
10. Shoup Park
11. McKenzie Park
12. Cuesta Park
13. Rengstorff Park
14. Shoreline Park

15. Memorial Park
16. Serra Park
17. Burgess Park
18. Nealon Park
19. Huddart Park
20. Las Palmas

67

Parks and Recreation

Palo Alto

The city of Palo Alto has more than thirty parks, a golf course, a children's museum/zoo, and theater, four swimming pools and three community centers.

Some facilities are available for rent to individuals and organizations. Group site reservations are available for Palo Alto residents at Mitchell and Rinconada Parks Reservations may be made at the Mitchell Park Community Center. 493-7674.

Palo Alto is sometimes referred to as a summer camp run by parents. The Palo Alto Department of Community Services offers a wide variety of preschool, children's, teens, special event, adults and seniors activities. You can find these activities listed in the *Enjoy* catalog. The catalog has three editions: Winter/Spring, Summer and Fall. For registration and catalog information please call 329-2261.

Rinconada Park   Rinconada Park is bordered by Middlefield, Emabarcadero and Newell. There are nine tennis courts, two playgrounds, picnic areas, shufflebooard courts, an adult swimming pool and a circular shaped three foot deep, children's pool. A children's library, a children's mini-zoo a children's museum and a children's theatre are all located within this Rinconada Park area. (415) 329-2487.

Mitchell Park   Located at 600 E. Meadow Drive, 329-2487. You can reserve picnic talbe areas for birthday parties. There are also handball courts, tennis courts, shuffleboard courts, a swimming pool and a wading pool.   Reservations required in spring and summer for picnic areas.

Johnson Park   Featured in the sand play area is a giant cement slide and a water faucet for sand play. The city is considering the idea of installing restrooms in this park.

Eleanor Pardee Park   Pardee Park is located on the corner of Center Drive and Newell Road in Palo Alto. The playground structures were renovated in late 1991 and offer two separate play areas.   The park is circled with a great pathway for strolling and features a rollerskating area.

Foothills Park   Foothills Park is reserved exclusively for Palo Alto residents and their guests. Proof of residency is required upon entry. (Driver's License with Palo Alto address). The park offers miles of trails in the foothills and plenty of picnic areas.

Briones Park   Located on Arastradero Road in Palo Alto. Two play areas, one offering a playstructure in the shape of a locomotive train. A slide runs from the top of the train to the sand. The other play area offers swings and a tunnel. The park has nice knolls and many picnic tables.

Chapter Five

Parks and Recreation

Peers Park   Peers Park is on Park Blvd which is off of El Camino as El Camino runs by the Stanford Campus. Peers Park has a large free form wooden climbing structure. There are also two merry-go-rounds, a gondola swing, large metal slide and swings. Two tennis courts, a basketball court and restrooms are also available.

Baylands Nature Preserve and Duck Pond
This preserve is often a favorite location for bird watching. More than 100 species of birds, including ducks, hawks and owls can be found there. This salt marsh is equipped with boardwalks offering visitors a close view of the wildlife. Slide shows, movies and workshops are scheduled on weekends. The boardwalks and pathways cover more than two miles of shoreline.

Neighborhood Parks

Los Altos

Heritage Oaks   Heritage Oaks Park is located on the corner of Miramonte and Portland which is off of the Foothill Expressway in Los Altos. This park is equipped with restrooms and a nice picnic area. There are two play areas; one with wooden climbing structures including a suspsension bridge, rope webbing and slides. The toddler area has a nice sandbox area with rock formations.

Shoup Park   A wonderfully secluded park with picnic tables, large grass area and two playstructure areas. Nice for large family gathering. Some footpaths that go through pretty Redwood grove along Adobe Creek. Two picnic tables provided on deck overlooking creek. Bathrooms and barbeques.

McKenzie Park   Tennis courts, picnic tables, barbeques and restrooms are a part of this park located on Altos Oaks Drive between Fremont and Miramonte Avenue. There are two tot-lot play areas and one large play area with a wooden climbing structure for older children.

Mountain View

Cuesta Park   Cuesta Park is a large park with many walkways and gentle grassy hills. Large picnic table area with barbeque available by reservation for large gatherings. Nice playstructure area. Bathrooms, barbeques and

Chapter Five

Neighbor-hood Parks

71

tennis courts are available. Located on corner of Cuesta and Grant Road in Mountain View between Foothill Expressway and El Camino Real.

Rengstorff Park   Rengstorff Park is located on the corner of Rengstorff and Central Expressway. The playground areas are enclosed and are divided into separate areas for older and younger children. The toddler playground has a variety of climbing structures in the sand. The older kids can climb on cement hills and a variety of metal sculptures. This park is also equipped with a large picnic area, a swimming pool and restrooms.

Shoreline Park   This is a large park surrounding Shoreline lake. Many bikepaths. Boathouse provides paddle boat and small sailboat rentals. Often an offshore breeze makes bikeriding more comfortable if you wear a windbreaker. Lots of green grass for picnicking or playing frisbee. Located on Shoreline Avenue in Mountain View, east of the 101.

Cupertino

Memorial Park   Memorial Park is located on the corner of Mary Avenue and Stevens Creek Boulevard in Cupertino. This park has a large duck pond with bridges and fountains. One playground features an Old West theme with a wooden structure simulating western storefronts. There's also a log tepee for climbing. The toddler area has a metal race car, and a merry-go-round.

Sunnyvale

Serra Park   Serra Park is located on the corner of Hollenbeck and Dalles in Sunnyvale. Serra Park has a super river boat theme to it's playstructure with suspension bridge, slide, and a county courthouse play area. The toddler play area has a nice sandbox. There are also restrooms, picnic areas, and tennis courts.

Menlo Park

Burgess Park   Located next to Menlo Park Library on Alma Street and Burgess Drive. This park has both sunny and shaded picnic tables. There are large playing fields and a large playstructure area.

Nealon Park   This park offers tennis courts, a softball field, a senior center, par course and a playground with a variety of playstructures. There are also restrooms and picnic areas. Nealon Park is on the west side of El Camino Avenue on Middle Avenue.

Woodside

Huddart Park   The park features hiking trails, picnic tables and barbeques. Take Sand Hill Road west through Woodside, then turn right on King's Mountain Road. (415) 851-0326.

Las Palmas Park   Located on the corner of Hyde Park and Russet in Sunnyvale, this park offers an island playground, a toddler playground next to the park lagoon and spray pool during the summer. Restrooms, picnic areas, and tennis courts are also available.

Berkeley

Adventure Playground   This playground is located at 225 University Avenue in Berkeley and is open on weekends and holidays from 11:00a.m.-4:00p.m. At this playground, there is a storage shed full of tools and scrap wood which the children use to build their own accomplishments. There are picnic tables and some interesting playstructures as well. (510) 644-8623.

San Francisco

Children's Playground   Located in Golden Gate Park which is the largest man-made park in the world, this playground offers many creative playstructures. Children's Playground was built in 1887 and was the first playground in a public park. Right next to the playground is the Carousel. You can find the playground on Bowling Green Drive between Martin Luther King Drive and John F. Kennedy Drive.

Stanford Recreation

Stanford Summer Sports Camps

Stanford offers sports camps in the summer for ages 7-17. Stanford offers; basketball, baseball soccer, gymnastics, swimming, tennis, and track. Adult classes are also offered in golf and volleyball. Each individual camp registration has a specific mailing address . For general information and to receive a brochure you can contact the Stanford Department of Athletics (415) 723-2591.

Stanford All Sports Camp   In the Roble Gym building you'll find the Physical Education & Recreation Department where you'll find the offices that will assist you for Stanford All Sports Camp. You'll also find information on youth sailing camps. For more information, please call (415) 723-3089.

Palo Alto Recreation

Albert Schultz Jewish Community Center
655 Arastradero Road
493-9400

Pacific Art League of Palo Alto
668 Ramona Street
321-3891

Baseball

Little League Baseball of Palo Alto, Inc.
P.O. Box 785
Palo Alto, CA 94302
Clubhouse Telephone 494-1933

Palo Alto Coed T-Ball League
City of Palo Alto Recreation
1305 Middlefield Road, 329-2487

Palo Alto Babe Ruth
Rick Beckwith, 852-9710

Bicycling

Western Wheelers Bicycle Club
P.O. Box 518
Palo Alto, CA 94302

Bowling

Palo Alto Bowl
4329 El Camino Real
948-1031 or 326-8010

Football

Palo Alto Knights/Pop Warner Football
Pat Farris 424-9888

Model Railroad Club

Jack Wall
854-5765

Softball

Palo Alto Bobby Sox
Dan Pritchard, 424-0469

Soccer

American Youth Soccer Organization
P.O. Box 1493
Palo Alto, CA 94302

Bay Area Women's Soccer
Judy Van Maasdam, 494-3673

California Youth Soccer Association
Ed Prentice, 494-3793

Palo Alto Adult Soccer
Carol Campbell, 851-1463

Silicon Valley Women's Soccer
Lynn Barber, 493-3856

Swimming

C.A.R. Swim Center
3864 Middlefield Road

Palo Alto Swim Club
Steve Power, (408) 268-6136

Rinconada Masters
Carol Remen 493-2930
Cindy Baxter 325-1578

Tennis

Palo Alto Tennis Club
(no lessons)
P.O. Box 60434
Palo Alto, CA 94306
854-6094

Ice Skating

Winterlodge
3009 Middlefield Road
493-4566

Menlo Park Recreation

Menlo Park offers many youth sports programs and has many nice facilities. Burgess Park offers picnic tables by reservation and Burgess Gym offers gymnastic classes. This gym is super for hosting private gymnastic class birthday parties. Noon-time parties are offered Tuesdays and Thursdays for 3-5 year olds. Recreation Department (415) 858-3472 and Gym 858-3480.

More recreation department listings are listed in the Appendix.

6

Chapter Six

State and National Parks

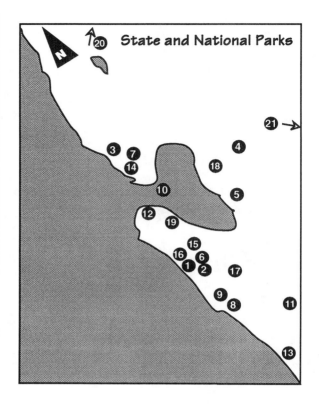

State and National Parks

1. Big Basin Redwoods
2. Butano State Park
3. Point Reyes Seashore
4. Mt. Diablo State Park
5. Knowland State Park
6. Portola State Park
7. Mt. Tamalpais State Park
8. Natural Bridges State Park
9. Henry Cowell State Park
10. Angel Island State Park
11. Pinnacles
12. GGNRA
13. Hearst Castle
14. Muir Woods

15. Sam McDonald Park
16. Pescadero Creek Park
17. Castle Rock Park
18. Charles Lee Tilden
19. Coyote Point Park
20. Shasta National Park
21. Yosemite National Park

80

State and National Parks

Big Basin Redwoods State Park

Located 30 miles south of Palo Alto in the Santa Cruz mountains. Take Highway 9, then west on Highway 236. Beautiful redwood park with hiking trails and camping. Very peaceful. 408-338-6132 or 408 438-4226.

Butano State Park

Five miles south of San Francisco you'll find 3,200 acres of redwood forests and chaparral. The park trails offer panoramic views of the Pacific Ocean and Ano Nuevo Island. Biking and camping also available.

Point Reyes National Seashore

This park extends from Leggett which is north of San Francisco southward to Sausalito. There are more than 60,000 acres included in this park. The national seashore features tidepools, secluded beaches, birds and mammals. Camping, bridle trails, biking, hiking, an earthquake trail, and freshwater lakes are inland. The Morgan Horse Ranch is a replica of a Miwok Indian village. There are four hike-in campgrounds and more than 120 miles of trails. (415) 663-1092.

Chapter Six

State and National Parks

81

Mt. Diablo State Park

The view from Mt. Diablo is from an elevation of almost 4,000 feet and on a clear day, looking in any direction you can see for more than 100 miles. The park covers almost 20,000 acres. It is located east of Interstate 680 on Mt. Diablo Road. (510) 837-2525.

Knowland State Park

Named after the publisher Joseph Knowland, from Oakland, this park is also a scientific reserve operated by the city of Oakland. There are botanical preserves and more than thirty shaded picnic areas and some playgrounds. Located off of Interstate 580 from the 98th Avenue exit. (510) 632-9523.

Portola State Park

Located on the beautiful coastal hillsides southwest of Palo Alto is Portola State Park. The park is a forest of more than 1,500 acres of Douglas fir and redwood trees. There are more than 100 picnic tables and many activites to do while visiting the park including more than 50 sites for overnight camping and many hiking trails.
You can reach the park from either Skyline Boulevard (State Highway 35) to Alpine Road to Portola Park Road or from La Honda Road (State Highway 84) to Pescadero Road to Alpine road to Portola Park Road.   (415) 948-9098.

Mount Tamalpais State Park

Mill Valley is at the base of Mt. Tamalpais.
Looking at the three peaked Mt. Tamalpais from
the southward view is said to look like the profile
of a sleeping Indian girl. The park is to the west of
Mill Valley. This 6,000 acre park offers bicycle
trails, hiking trails and many spectacular views of
Marin County. In the spring, the Mountain
Theater presents plays and musical productions.
(415) 388-2070.

Natural Bridges Beach State Park

In October and again in March in a grove of
eucalyptus trees in the park, Monarch butterflies
gather. The monarchs may travel up to three
thousand miles to arrive here and on the second or
third Saturday in October, the park holds a Welcome Back Monarchs Day. The park is named
after the natural bridge of land carved by the
pounding surf. The arch broke in 1980. Tidepool
observing is a feature of the park at low tide and
park naturalist guided tidepool tours are available. For your safety, swimming is said to be
unsafe and no lifeguards are provided. Located in
Santa Cruz. (408) 423-4609.

Henry Cowell Redwoods State Park

In 1953, Henry Cowell gave California the land
which is mostly a grove of redwoods and Pon-
derosa pines. The San Lorenzo River runs
through the park. Most of the park is semi-
wilderness. There are hiking and equestrian trails.

83

Overnight campsights are available by reservation. The park is just south of Felton. Take
California Highway 9 to Graham Hill Road.
(408) 335-4598.

Angel Island State Park

This island is about 700 acres and once served as
a military base from 1850 to 1946, an immigration
camp and a war-prison. Tours of theses areas are
available. To reach the island, you can take a
ferry from Tiburon or a charter boat from Pier 43
at Fisherman's Wharf in San Francisco. Picnicking, bike riding and hiking are great activities on
the island.

Shasta National Recreational Area

The Whiskeytown-Shasta-Trinity National Recreation Area and National Forest offers a range of
outdoor activities. Three impounded lakes are
within this area; Whiskeytown Lake, (916) 241-
6584, is a popular spot for canoeing and sailing,
Clair Engle Lake and Shasta Lake. Shasta Lake,
(916) 275-1587, is manmade with more than 300
miles of shoreline and offers plenty of fishing and
boating. The Lake Shasta Caverns, (916) 238-
2341 are beautiful limestone and marble caves
that can be seen on tours. The Shasta Dam can
be seen from a vista point overlooking the dam.
The dam has the highest overflow spillway in the
world with a water drop height of three times the
height of Niagara Falls. (916) 275-1554.

Yosemite National Park

This spectacular national park offers camp-grounds, fishing, horseback riding, hiking, etc. Make reservations well in advance by calling: Park Service Camping (209)-4252-4848; Wawona Hotel operated by the Yosemite Park and Curry Co. 209-372-0264. The landscape of this park isunusual with some of the territory displaying the snowy peaks of the Sierra Nevada mountains and other areas showing rolling hills and meadows with two rivers carving a gorge through the northern half of the park. Waterfalls and tree groves also mark this unusually beautiful park.

Pinnacles National Monument

Located south of Salinas near Soledad are the Pinnacles. The area is the remains of volcanic action and underground are caves. There are many interconnecting trails. (408) 389-4526. Chaparral Campground offers year round camp-sites.

Golden Gate National Recreation Area

This park covers more than 74,000 acres and is the largest urban national park. The MUNI system of San Francisco offers transportation to many of the park's attractions.

Golden Gate Promenade Covering more than three miles is this beautiful waterfront pathway with scenic views of the oceanfront. The pathway stretches from Fort Point to Aquatic Park.

Hearst Castle/San Simeon

Many different tours of the late William Randolph Hearst's estate are available. There are more than one hundred acres of gardens, pools, terraces and guest houses. Reservations may be made through the California State Parks System phone number 800-444-7275.

Muir Woods

Just over the Golden Gate Bridge off of SR 1 right along the coast is Muir Woods. These woods are filled with redwood groves. The trails are great for hiking. There are more than twenty miles of trails which vary in length from a half mile to two miles. Camping and picnicking are not permitted. The park is named after naturalist John Muir. There is a coffee shop, visitor and interpretive center. (415) 388-2595.

Sam McDonald Park

Named after a former Stanford janitor who acquired the land and then donated the more than four hundred acres to Stanford. San Mateo Conty then acquired the land and it is now used for hikers and campers. The Hiker's Hut can be reserved for overnight camping. (415) 363-4021.

Pescadero Creek County Park

For decades this area was heavily logged. Now the old logging roads are used by backpackers, hikers, and mountain bikers. (415) 747-0403.

Castle Rock State Park

Located along Skyline Boulevard in Los Gatos is Castle Rock Park. This park is primarily for hikers. There are many panoramic views along the hiking trails and some areas are known to local rock climbers. Castle Rock is about eighty feet in height. Castle Rock Falls is about a one hundred foot waterfall and can be observed from a platform. (408) 867-2952.

Charles Lee Tilden Regional Park

This two thousand acre park is situated above Berkeley in the East Bay. The park offers an antique merry-go-round, a nature center, a petting farm, a miniature steam train, pony rides, a golf course, botanic garden, lake swimming and many miles of trails. The Environmental Center offers a naturalist program and many displays about the East Bay's natural history. (510) 531-9300.

Coyote Point Recreation Area

Located along the bay just south of the San Francisco International Airport in San Mateo, this park features the Coyote Point Museum for Environmental Education. The museum emphasizes the environmental relationships within the San Francisco Bay Area. The museum is known for its unique way of presenting the eight biotic communities in the San Francisco Bay Area. The park offers many picnic areas, some available by reservation. (415) 363-4021. Museum (415) 342-7755.

**Chapter
Six**

**Bike
Paths
and
Hiking
Trails**

Bike Paths and Hiking Trails

Many trails in the Bay Area parks are shared by hikers, joggers, equestrians and bicyclists. Bicyclists are required to yield to pedestrians, hikers and equestrians. Some parks have speed limits for bicyclists. Where bicyclists are allowed on all park trails, they are required to wear bike helmets.

Mountain biking actually became popular in the 1970's and started in the Marin County area. After many problematic events with bikers and hikers and equestrians, many parks enforce strict regulations that govern all bike use.

There are many suitable trails throughout the San Francisco Bay Area for biking. Palo Alto, Menlo Park and Los Altos have special bike lanes yielding sections of the city roads just for bicyclists. The Stanford campus can be travelled completely by bike as there is a paved bike path winding along the perimeter of the campus. Foothill Expressway, Junipero Serra Boulevard have well marked bike lanes along the side of the road. Sand Hill Road and roadways in Woodside also offer bike lanes. Many parks in the Bay Area offer bike paths.

Several biking and hiking books are listed in the resource/bibliography section of this book. These books can help provide you with more specifics on the paths mentioned in this section including maps, topographic information and general information about trail, road and traffic conditions.

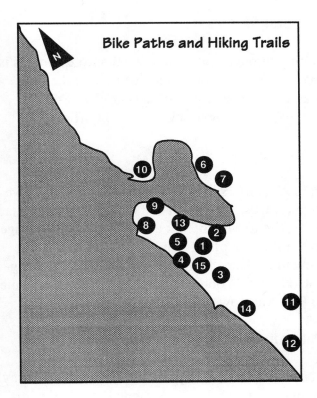

Bike Paths and Hiking Trails

1. Stanford Campus
2. Palo Alto Baylands
3. Arastradero Road
4. Sawyer's Camp Trail
5. Bicycle Sunday
6. Tilden Park
7. Redwood Regional Park
8. Golden Gate Park
9. Golden Gate Promenade
10. Mt. Tamalpais
11. Alum Rock Park
12. Henry Coe State Prk
13. Coyote Point Park
14. Rancho San Antonio

15. Portola Valley Loop

The Stanford Campus

Biking through and around the Stanford campus is made easier with the extensive paved bike trails that loop the perimeter of the campus. Some of the roads on campus are closed to traffic.

Palo Alto

Palo Alto offers many painted bike lanes and five bike bridges. The north end of Waverly connects Palo Alto to Menlo Park as well as the bike bridge to Menlo Park off of Sand Hill Road west of the Ronald McDonald House. Bryant Street is designated as a bike boulevard from University Avenue to East Meadow Avenue.

Palo Alto Baylands /Mt. View Shoreline

The Bayfront Trail is paved and winds all the way around the more than one hundred acres of wildlife sanctuary. This same trail continues into the Shoreline in Mountain View. There are more than six miles of nearly level paved bike paths. It is often windy with the off shore breeze.

Arastradero Road and Foothill Expressway

Near Gunn High School there are three paved bike paths that begin in the very busy intersection of Arastradero and Foothill Expressway. The **Palo Alto - Los Altos Bike Path** begins at Gunn High and ends on Mercedes Avenue. Round trip it is only about a mile and a half. **Bol Park Trail** On the west end of Gunn High School you can

90

pick up this paved path which winds along an old Southern Pacific railroad route. The path offers views of the foothills, open space and many oak trees. The path ends at Hanover Street . Round trip it is about two and one half miles. The **Arastradero Bike Path** round trip is about three and one half miles. It follows alongside Arastradero Road for more than a mile and then alongside Deer Creek. It ends at Purissima Road in Los Altos Hills.

Sawyer's Camp Trail

The smooth paved well maintained condition of this path attracts rollerbladers, joggers and families on bikes. The trail runs alongside portions of Crystal Springs Reservoir and San Andreas Lake. Around the four mile mark is a climb of about one hundred feet to the San Andreas Dam. Take the Bunker Hill Road exit from Interstate 280. Go west to Skyline Boulevard. There will be a sign indicating "Historic Sawyer's Camp Road". A round trip ride along the trail is about twelve miles. (415) 363-4020.

Bicycle Sunday

Three Sundays a month are reserved for Bicycle Sunday from March through October. A portion of the two lane smoothly paved Canada Road is closed to automobiles. The bike ride goes through the San Francisco State Fish and Game Refuge and also passes the Filoli estate. For a Bicycle Sunday brochure, call (415) 363-4020.

Tilden Park

Biking is allowed on Wildcat Creek Trail and Loop Road (between Wildcat Creek Trail and Central Park Drive. Biking is not permitted on any other roads or on any other trails. (510) 525-2233.

Redwood Regional Park

Located in the East Bay this park permits biking along the East and West Ridge and Canyon trails. Biking is also permitted along the Stream Trail up until Trail's End picnic area. (510) 531-9043.

Golden Gate Park

Every Sunday, the east end of Golden Gate Park is closed to automobiles so bicyclists, walkers and rollerbladers can use the roads freely.

Golden Gate Promenade

The promenade route runs between Aquatic Park and Fort Point. Beginning at Fort Mason and going west you'll pass by San Francisco's yacht harbor. Continuing along this route, you'll pass the Marina Green. Later you'll pass the waterfront area of the Presidio and Crissy Field and ending at Fort Point.

Mt. Tamalpais

There are permitted routes for bicyclists on Mt. Tamalpais. Bikes are permitted only on roads, not trails. The Marin Municipal Water District office in Corte Madera provides a bike map along with a code of regulations. The map is essential if you plan to bike on Mount Tamalpais. (415) 924-4600.

Alum Rock Park

Alum Rock Park is located in San Jose just off of highway 101 on the Alum Rock Avenue exit. The Creek Trail and the North Rim Trail are open to bicyclists. Paved roads in this park are also open for bike riding. (408) 259-5477.

Henry W. Coe State Park

This park consists of more than fifty thousand acres. This park is not for the beginner, but for those experienced bikers. Many of the acres are old ranches accompanied by old ranch roads many of which are open to cyclists. Bikes are not allowed in the Orestimga Wilderness. (408) 779-2728. Park is located at south end of Santa Clara off County near Morgan Hill. East Dunne Avenue Exit off of highway 101.

93

Coyote Point Park

Located along the San Francisco Bay shoreline, this park has about one mile of a paved path that runs along the edge of the park. Actually the Coyote Point Park paved paths are a part of the Bayfront Trail which runs along the shorefront from the Belmont Slough northward. Portions of this pathway are temporarily closed. However, the loop from East Third Avenue through the park is about a four mile ride.

Rancho San Antonio

This park provides many trails for hikers and equestrians and a paved bicycle path for bicyclists. The park entrance is off of Cristo Rey Drive which is just west of Interstate 280. From 280 take Foothill Boulevard south. Santa Clara County Parks and Recreation Department. (408) 358-3741.

The Portola Valley /Stanford Loop

The Portola Valley Loop begins at the Stanford stadium, then to Campus Drive East to Junipero Serra to Alpine to Portola Road to Sand Hill Road and back to West Campus Drive. It is about a fifteen mile ride round trip with a steady climb on Alpine Road. Another version of the loop is to take Junipero Serra to Page Mill to Old Page Mill to Arastradero Road and then left onto Alpine Road.

7

Chapter Seven

Area Restaurants

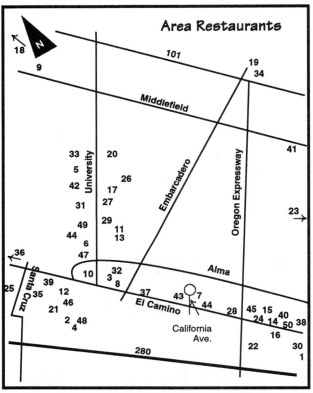

Area Restaurants

1. Armadillo Willy's
2. California Cafe
3. California Cafe
4. Fresh Choice
5. The Gatehouse
6. The Good Earth
7. Hearts Cafe
8. Hobee's
9. Late for the Train
10. MacArthur Park
11. Maddalena's
12. The Oasis
13. Peninsula Creamery
14. Sizzler Steack House
15. Talbott's
16. The Fish Market
17. Pearl's Oyster Bar
18. Pete's Harbor House

19. Scott's Seafood
20. Theo's
21. Azur
22. Chez Louis
23. Chez TJ
24. Panach e
25. Capriccio
26. Florentine
27. Osteria
28. Olive Garden
29. Ramona's
30. Chef Chu's
31. China Delight
32. King Chuan
33. Mandarin Gourmet
34. Ming's
35. Su Hong
36. Chevy's

37. Casa Isabel
38. Compadres
39. Applewood
40. Domino's
41. Murphy's
42. Pizza A GoGo
43. Ramona's Too
44. Round Table
45. Thai Garden
46. Siam Garden
47. Nataraja
48. Gaylord
49. Miyake
50. Fuki-Sushi

Area Restaurants

American Food

Armadillo Willy's BBQ
1031 N. San Antonio Road
Los Altos (415) 941-2922.
Baby back ribs, Texas BBQ. Reasonable.

California Cafe
Stanford Barn
700 Welch Rd.
Palo Alto (415)325-2233.
President Clinton dined at the California Cafe
in Los Gatos. Menu offers variety of salads and
main entrees. Reasonable.

Cook Book Restaurant
127 Town and Country Village
Palo Alto (415) 321-7500.
Omelets, salads, sandwiches. Reasonable.

Fresh Choice
Stanford Shopping Center next to B of A.
600 Santa Cruz Avenue in Menlo Park
1105 W El Camino Real, Sunnyvale
333 Moffett Pard Drive, Sunnyvale
Huge all you can eat health food salad, soup,
pasta, bakery, dessert bar. Reasonable.
Kids five and under free.

The Gatehouse
265 Lytton Avenue
Palo Alto (415) 326-9449.
Patio dining. Expensive.

**Chapter
Seven**

**Area
Restaurants**

97

The Good Earth
185 University Avenue
Palo Alto, 321-9449.
Vegetarian specials, bakery. Reasonable.

Hearts Cafe
201 California Avenue
Palo Alto (415) 322-1285.
Casual dining, fresh pasta and desserts.
Reasonable.

Hobee's
67 Town and Country Village,
Palo Alto (415) 327-4711
4224 El Camino Real,
Palo Alto (415)856-6124
Health food restaurant with breakfast
served all day. Reasonable.

Late for the Train
Brunches, etc.
150 Middlefield (and Willow)
Menlo Park, 321-6124

MacArthur Park
27 University Avenue
Palo Alto (415) 321-9990.
Baby back ribs (award winning). Expensive.

Maddalena's
544 Emerson
Palo Alto (415) 326-6082
Upscale busy restaurant with private dining
rooms. Expensive.

The Oasis
241 El Camino Real
Menlo Park (415) 326-8896.
A long time Stanford hangout for hamburgers.
Reasonable.

Peninsula Creamery
Serving breakfast, lunch, milkshakes and fries
since 1923. On the corner of Hamilton and
Emerson. 323-3131.

Sizzler Family Steak House
3375 El Camino Real
Palo Alto (415) 493-0153.
All you can eat salad bar and child's buffet.
Reasonable.

Talbott's Restaurant
463 California Avenule
Palo Alto (415) 326-7762.
Casual atmoshpere, sandwiches, salads.
Reasonable.

Seafood

The Fish Market
3150 El Camino Real
Palo Alto (415) 493-9188
Casual dining, fresh fish. Reasonable.

Pearl's Oyster Bar
535 Ramona Avenue
Palo Alto, 328-2722
Patio dining with seafood and entertainment.
Reasonable to Expensive.

Pete's Harbor House
on Uccelli at the end of Whipple
Redwood City (415) 365-1386
Steak and seafood dining. Reasonable to
Expensive.

Scott's Seafood Grill and Bar
corner of East Embarcadero and East Bayshore
Palo Alto (415) 856-1046
Fresh fish, steak and lobster. Expensive (although
first seating is less expensive)

Theo's
546 University Avenue
Palo Alto (415) 322-1272
Menu changes weekly. Fresh seafood daily.
Reasonable.

French

Azur
646 Santa Cruz Avenue
Menlo Park (415) 327-3140.
Continental French cooking. Reasonable.

Chez Louis
4170 El Camino
Palo Alto (415) 493-1660
Casual French atmosphere.
Reasonable to Expensive.

Chez T J
938 Villa
Mountain View (415) 964-7466
Prix fixe menus every two weeks. Expensive.

Panache Contemporary French Restaurant
3740 El Camino Real
Palo Alto (415) 494-0700
Patio dining. Expensive.

Italian

Capriccio
4546 El Camino Real near San Antonio Road
Los Altos (415) 941-1855
Fresh pasta. Reasonable.

Florentine Restaurant
560 Waverly   Palo Alto (415) 326-5295
4546 El Camino Los Altos (415) 949-1235
2525 El Camino Redwood City (415) 365-0444
1118 Castro Mountain View (4150 961-6543
Gourmet homemade pasta. Reasonable.

Osteria
On corner of Hamilton and Ramona
Palo Alto (415) 328-570
Formal dining, homemade pasta. Reasonable.

Olive Garden
2515 El Camino Real near California
Palo Alto (415) 326-5673.
Homemade pasta, fresh salads. Reasonable.

Ramona's
541 Ramona in downtown Palo Alto
(415) 326-2220. Homemade soups, gourmet
pasta, fresh salad bar, New York style pizza.
Since 1976. Reasonable.

Chinese Food

Chef Chu's
1067 N. San Antonio
Los Altos (415) 948-2696
Formal dining with reasonable price.

China Delight
203 University Avenue
Palo Alto (415) 326-6065
Mandarin and Szechuan cuisine. Reasonable.

King Chuan Restaurant
75 Town and Country Village
Palo Alto (415) 323-6550
Family style dining. Takeout. Reasonable.

Mandarin Gourmet
420 Ramona Street
Palo Alto (415) 328-8898.
Formal dining. Szechuan and Mandarin cuisine.
Reasonable to Expensive.

Ming's
1700 Embarcadero Road
Palo Alto (415) 856-7700
Dim Sum, Mandarin, Cantonese and Szechuan
cuisine. Since 1956. Formal dining. Expensive to
Very Expensive.

Su Hong
1039 El Camino
Menlo Park (425) 323-6852.
Take out available. Inexpensive.

Mexican Food

Chevy's Mexican Restaurant
2907 El Camino
Redwood City (415) 367-6892
204 S Mathilda in Sunnyvale, 408 737-7395
Fresh Mex-Reasonable

Casa Isabel
2434 Park Boulevard near California
Palo Alto (415) 328-3102
Reasonable.

Compadres
3877 El Camino Real
Palo Alto (415) 858-1141
Large portions, variety. Reasonable.

Pizza

Palo Alto has plenty of places to order pizza either
to eat in or take out. There are privately owned
pizza parlors as well as some of the major chains.

Applewood Inn
1001 El Camino Real
Menlo Park (415) N323-3486
Thick crust with plenty of toppings. Reasonable.

Domino's Pizza
240B Cambridge Avenue
Palo Alto (415) 326-6552.
Thirty minute delivery. Reasonable.

Murphy's Take and Bake
2730 Middlefield Road
Palo Alto (415) 328-5200.
You order your pizza toppings then take the pizza
home and bake it. Pizza prices are very
reasonable.

Pizza A Go Go
335 University Avenue
Palo Alto (415) 322-8100.
A variety of pizzas including vegetarian pizzas
and pizza by the slice. Reasonable.

Ramona's Too
2313 Birch Street
Palo Alto (415) 326-2220
Many varieties of pizza. Reasonable.

Round Table Pizza
Four locations in Palo Alto
Alma (415) 494-2928
California Avenue (415) 322-0111
Colorado (415) 322-5914
University (415) 322-2893
Many other locations. Reasonable to expensive.

Thai

Thai Garden
4329 El Camino Real
Palo Alto (415)949-5259
Thai Noodles, lemon grass soups.
Reasonable.

Siam Garden
1143 Crane
Menlo Park (415) 854-0156
Dinners only. Reasonable.

Indian

Nataraja Restaurant
117 University Avenue
Palo Alto (415) 321-6161
Candlelight dinners, salad bar.
Reasonable to expensive.

Gaylord India Restaurant
317 Stanford Shopping Center
Palo Alto (415) 326-8761
North Indian dishes. Expensive.

Japanese

Miyake Japanese Restaurant
261 University Avenue
Palo Alto (4150 323-9449.
Very lively restaurant. Sushi. Reasonable.

Fuki-Sushi
4119 El Camino Real
Palo ALto (415) 494-8393.
Family style, sushi bar. Reasonable to expensive.

Delicatessens

Draeger's Supermarket
1010 University Drive, Menlo Park
(415) 688-0686
342 1st Street, Los Altos
(415) 948-7204. Bakery and deli on first floor.
Second floor has coffee and luncheon area for
quick deli sandwiches and fresh pasta. Ready
made deli sandwiches are reasonably priced.

John's Market
Town and Country Village
Embarcadero and El Camino in Palo Alto.
(415) 321-0420. Sandwiches made to order are
huge and very reasonably priced. Chinese take
out too.

J.J. and F. Food Store
520 College Avenue in Palo Alto.
(415) 857-0901. A variety of fresh seafood can
be purchased from this deli.

Max's Opera Cafe
Stanford Shopping Center
(415)323-6297
New York style deli. Also a restaurant with
singing waiters at night.

Stanford Delicatessen
Stanford Shopping Center
(415) 328-3354. A wide variety of meats to
choose from.

Whole Foods Market
774 Emerson in Palo Alto
(415) 326-8676. Prices tend to be a little higher, but it is certainly worth the visit to see the health foods offered in the deli, bakery and produce market. Many great items to choose from.

Woodside Deli
1453 Woodside Road
Redwood City (415) 369-4235.
Many cheeses to choose from. Reasonably priced.

Entertainment

Entertainment in the Bay Area includes many options from San Francisco to San Jose. Many of the grand hotels in downtown San Francisco offer jazz and dancing nightly. Downtown San Jose offers many night clubs with musical and comedy shows. The Shoreline Amphitheater in Mountain View and Villa Montalvo in Saratoga bring many well known musicians.

Located in Saratoga is the beautiful Paul Masson Mountain Winery. The Masson Summer Series offers a wide variety of performances including classical, popular and jazz musicians. The Villa Montalvo Center for the Arts is of a Mediterranean design and offers a beautiful view of the surrounding Saratoga hills. The center offers both theater and concerts. (410) 741-3421.

In Mountain View is the Shoreline Amphitheater which brings in many world famous musicians and singers. (415) 962-1000.

The Cow Palace in Daly City (415) 469-6000 and the Circle Star Theater in Redwood City (415) 366-7100 both offer a calendar of events that include special trade shows as well as celebrities

There are also many night spots to choose from in the North Beach section of San Francisco. North Beach extends from the Telegraph Hill area to the waterfront. Club Fugasi located at 678 Green Street, (415) 421-4222, offers the musical revue *Beach Blanket Babylon* performed cabaret style.

108

Comedy Clubs

Rooster T. Feathers
157 W. El Camino
Sunnyvale (408) 736-0921.
Both national and local comedy acts.

Improv
401 Mason
San Francisco (415) 441-7787.
Local comedy acts.

Movie Theaters

Century Cinema 10 Theaters
1500 N. Shoreline
Mountain View (415) 960-0970.
Take Shoreline Blvd east exit off of 101.

Century Park 12 Theaters
557 E. Bayshore
Redwood City (415) 365-9000.
Take Whipple Avenue exit east off of 101.

Palo Alto Square Theaters 1 & II
Southwest corner of Pagemill and El Camino
Palo Alto (415) 493-1160.

Stanford Theater
221 University
Palo Alto (415) 324-3700

UA Redwood 6 Theaters
305 Walnut
Redwood City (415) 367-9090

Chapter Seven

Movie Theaters

Performing Arts

Chapter Seven

Performing Arts

San Francisco offers an abundance of theatrical and musical activity. The **San Francisco Ballet Company** performs at the Civic Center and the War Memorial Opera House. The **San Francisco Symphony** holds performances year round in Davies Symphony Hall and seasonal performances at Stern Grove, a wooded natural amphitheater. There are many theaters downtown such as the American Conservatory Theater, the Geary Theater and the Golden Gate Theater.

The South Bay offers the **San Jose Symphony** with performances at the Flint Center (408) 287-7383, **Opera San Jose** at the Montgomery Theater, (408) 288-8882, the **San Jose Chamber Music Society**, (408) 286-5111, the San Jose Dance Theater, (408) 293-5665 and the **San Jose Cleveland Ballet** with performances at the Center for the Performing Arts, (408) 288-2820.

The California Youth Symphony (415) 325-6666, the **Palo Alto Chamber Orchestra**, (415) 856-3848 and the **El Camino Youth Symphony**, (415) 327-3369 are located in Palo Alto. These orchestras consist of young people ages six to high school and performances throughout the school year are offered at Foothill College in Los Altos, the Cultural Center in Palo Alto, the Flint Center in Cupertino and the San Mateo Performing Arts Center.

8

Chapter
Eight

San Francisco

The Waterfront

Jefferson Street runs along the water. This water-front area harbors fishing boats and many fine seafood restaurants. You'll also find many open markets along this waterfront area where you can buy freshly cooked Dungeness crab and some of San Francisco's famous sour dough bread.

Fisherman's Wharf

Chapter Eight

The Water-front

Fisherman's Wharf offers many open fish markets where you can buy fresh shrimp or crab cocktails. You'll also find; Ripley's "Believe it or Not" Museum (415) 771-6188 and the Wax Museum at Fisherman's Wharf (415) 885-4975.

Pier 39

Just to the east of Fisherman's Wharf is Pier 39. Pier 39 is a split level pier with more than ten fine restaurants and more than 100 specialty shops. Live entertainment can be found in the center of the pier offered by street performers. The view from many of the restaurants is spectacular as you look out over the marina and the boats sailing on San Francisco Bay.

Aquatic Park

Just east of Fort Mason is Aquatic Park which is one of San Francisco's sandy beaches. The park also contains green lawns often frequented by street performers, and a curving pier.

The Cannery

The Cannery is100 years old in 1994. Originally
it was built as a plant for canning peaches owned
by the Del Monte Company. However, the
interior of this plant has been converted to a
marketplace with a European-style. The patio
often hosts many street performers such as musicians, mimes, magicians and jugglers. Located
near Fisherman's Wharf on Leavenworth Street.
(415) 771-3112.

San Francisco International Toy Museum

Located in The Cannery at 2801 Leavenworth
Street. This is a hands on museum especially
designed for kids. There are many toys to play
with including a fancy Brio wooden train set and
track. (415) 441-TOYS.

Ghirardelli Square

Ghirardelli Square houses what used to be a
chocolate factory along with more than sixty
shops and restaurants. Like Fisherman's Wharf,
you will find many street performers offering free
entertainment.

Red & White Fleet

Cruises around the bay, Marineworld Africa USA,
Alcatraz, etc. Located at Pier 41 at Fisherman's
Wharf. 1-800-445-8880 or (415) 546-2896.

San Francisco Sights

Golden Gate Park

Chapter Eight

San Francisco Sights

This national park is the largest in the world. The park offers more than 1,000 acres of lakes, flowers, pathways and meadows. (415) 666-7200. Stow Lake offers boat rentals. Spreckels Lake is a great place to test model boats. Feeding the ducks is another great past time at Golden Gate Park. Visit the **California Academy of the Sciences** and see the **Steinhart Aquarium** (415) 221-5100, to see more than two hundred fish tanks and an entry courtyard inhabited by alligators and crocodiles. The **Morrison Planetarium** (415) 750-7141 is a special sky theater offering shows about the stars and galaxies. **Laserium** (415) 750-7138 offers a laser show for children ages six and older. The **Conservatory** (415) 558-3983 offers a display of flowers and the **Japanese Tea Garden** where you can carefully climb on a moon bridge and see a large Buddha statue. The cherry blossoms are in full bloom in late March or early April (415) 668-0909.

Chinatown

Located near Union Square on Grant Avenue between Columbus and Bush. Many Chinese restaurants, stores and teahouses can be found in this area. The **Golden Gate Fortune Cookies Company** is located in Chinatown on Ross Alley (near Washington and Grant). Here you can see just how fortune cookies are made and watch the workers place the fortunes inside the cookies.

Museum of Modern Art

This museum conducts educational art programs for preschool aged through young teens. Located in the War Memorial Veteran Building on the corner of Van Ness and McAllister near City Hall. (415) 863-8800.

Museum of Modern Mythology

This is a very amusing museum that features advertising memoribilia including media characters such as the Pillsbury Dough Boy. Located at 693 Mission Street. (415) 546-0202.

M. H. De Young Memorial Museum

Every Saturday from 10:30a.m.-12:00p.m. a special children's art class is held on a drop in basis for children ages 7 -12. The museum is located in Golden Gate Park in San Francisco. (415) 750-3658.

Exploratorium

This science museum utilizes the senses of sight, sound and touch. It is located in the restored Palace of Fine Arts. 3601 Lyon Street at Marina Blvd. (415) 561-0360. There are more than five hundred exhibits, each one being interactive with some kind of hands on demonstration of the sciences. Admission is free the first Wednesday of every month.

Lombard Street

This winding cobblestone street descends into the North Beach area of San Francisco with a series of "S" shaped curves and is known as the crookedest street in the world.

Coit Tower

Located on Telegraph Hill and built in 1933 somewhat in the shape of a firehose nozzle. It was built to memorialize the volunteer firefighters. It was built in 1933 and has an elevator which takes you to an observation deck. (415) 391-1188.

San Francisco Zoo

Located on Sloat Blvd. and 45th Avenue close to Oceran Beach. The San Francisco Zoo includes Monkey Island (scheduled for renovation) where spider monkeys live and a very large gorilla habitat. There's also a Children's Zoo (small entrance fee) with a petting area and a special Insect Zoo. (415) 753-7083 (tape) or 753-7080.

Palace of the Legion of Honor

Located in Lincoln Park near the Exploratorium. The museum houses French art and culture as well as a collection of medieval paintings, sculptures, prints and drawings. Rodin's *Thinker* is in the entry. Undergoing renovation through 1994.

Fort Mason

Located along the waterfront near Fisherman's Wharf is Fort Mason, a converted army post which now serves as the headquarters for the Golden Gate National Recreation Area. Fort Mason houses many museums including; the Craft and Folk Art Museum, African-American Historical and Cultural Society, Mexican Museum, Museo Italo American, and the Cable Car Museum. Greens Restaurant in Fort Mason offers a great vegetarian menu and fantastic views while dining.

Cable Car Barn Viewing House

Although the Cable Car Museum is closed indefintely, the barn is open and you can still view cable cars from the car barn. The brick cable car barn was built in 1887 and all of the cable car lines are run by the revolving wheels in this barn. (415) 474-1887.

Japan Town

Bounded by Geary, Laguna, Fillmore and Post is Japantown (Nihonmachi) where more than ten thousand people of Japanese decent reside. **Japan Center** located at Buchanan and Post is a huge complex of restaurants, sushi bars, theaters and stores. The Peace Pagoda is the center for ceremonies including the Cherry Blossom Festival in the spring.

Cliff House

Built right on a cliff overlooking the Pacific Ocean is the Cliff House, first built in 1896 and restored in 1909. It now houses an old fashioned amusement arcade with more than one hundred coin operated machines, a museum and a restaurant. Located at 1090 Point Lobos Avenue (415) 386-1170.

Josephine D. Randall Junior Museum

This is a children's museum. Art, craft and hobby classes are offered. The museum has an animal room with an area for petting small animals. Located on Museum Way and Roosevelt way in Twin Peaks. (415) 554-9600.

Fort Point National Historic Site

Built in 1861 to protect the entrance to San Francisco Bay. Located under the south end of the Golden Gate Bridge. Tours are available through out the week and demonstrations are given on weekends. The rangers are dressed in Civil War uniforms. Slide shows are also given as well as a movie describing the construction of the Golden Gate Bridge. (415) 556-1693.

Alcatraz Island

From 1934 to 1963 Alcatraz was a federal prison where the toughest criminals were held, including Al Capone. Robert Kennedy closed Alcatraz in 1963 and now you can tour the prison and the island. The Red and White Fleet runs boats regularly to Alcatraz from Pier 41.

Hyde Street Pier

Between Fisherman's Wharf and Aquatic Beach is the Hyde Street Pier which is also where the cable car line ends and where you can visit many vintage ships at the **San Francisco Maritime National Historical Park.**

Balclutha

This square-rigged sailing vessel with three masts is anchored at Hyde Street Pier along with the **Thayer** and the **Eureka**. You can board each ship for a self guided tour. Knot tying demonstrations are often presented.

Ansel Adams Center

Five galleries with one of ongoing displays of the photography works of Ansel Adams. Also features rotating exhibits on the history of photography. Located at 250 Fourth Street. Free on the first Tuesday of each month. (415) 495-7000.

**Chapter
Eight**

**San
Francisco
Sights**

119

Shopping in San Francisco

There are many places to shop in San Francisco as it is a world marketplace. Union Square, Crocker Galleria, Union Street and the San Francisco Shopping Centre offer a variety of upscale famous stores while south of Market Street offers many discount factory outlets for clothing, accessories and toys.

Waterfront Shopping

Chapter Eight

Shopping in San Francisco

Fisherman's Wharf and **Pier 39** offer many souvenir shops. Located on Taylor Street near Fisherman's Wharf is **Cost Plus Imports** which stocks a great variety of housewares, baskets, and inexpensive toys. **Ghirardelli Square** is located near the Hyde Street Pier. **The Cannery** is between Fisherman's Wharf and Ghirardelli Square. **The Cannery** is a large brick complex that used to house the Del Monte Fruit Cannery and now houses specialty shops and restaurants.

Embarcadero Center

Located between Battery and the Ferry Building is Embarcadero Center with the Embarcadero Garage available for parking. Embarcadero Center is three level four block complex with outdoor cafes, boutiques, specialty shops and restaurants covering more than ten acres. The Hyatt Regency is located at one end of the complex and the Park Hyatt at the other.

San Francisco Shopping Center

This center offers nine floors of shops with the top five floors being occupied by Nordstrom's Department Store. There are more than seventy specialty shops and boutiques and several restaurants to choose from. The center is located on Powell and Market streets.

Crocker Galleria

This three level building is located in the financial district downtown and is named after Charles Crocker. Mr. Crocker and Leland Stanford were two of four men who built the Central Pacific Railroad. The galleria is bound by Sutter, Montgomery, Kearny and Post. It offers more than forty boutiques, many restaurants, two rooftop gardens, all under a glass dome.

Victorian Homes

Just south of the Presidio and west of the Pacific Heights area of San Francisco is a four block area surrounding Sacramento Street that has Victorian Homes some of which house coffee shops, specialty shops and art galleries.

Union Square Area

There are many fine department stores in this area including Gumps, Saks, Macy's and the Crocker Galleria. Each Christmas season, these stores offer very attractive window displays and the center of the square displays a huge Christmas tree. The area is bounded by Powell, Post, Geary and Stockton Streets and Union Square received its name as a result of pro-Union demonstrations that were held there in 1860. Sutter Street offers many art and antique shops.

Union Street

Literally torn in two in the great 1906 earthquake, the street now offers many restored Victorians that house restaurants, book shops, and many specialty shops and even shopping malls. There are many flower filled courtyards to browse through.

Factory Outlets South of Market

Many factory outlets are located in the area of Third, Bryant Street and Brannon Street as well as the Yerba Buena Square on 5th and Howard, all south of Market street. There are more than fifteen outlets located at the Six-Sixty Center on 3rd Street offering discounts on accessories, clothing and shoes. Designer factory outlets can also be found.

San Francisco Restaurants

San Francisco may have easily more than two thousand restaurants. The following listings are restaurants that have been in San Francisco for many years and continue to be popular. Reservations are strongly recommended for the larger restaurants.

Cafe Latte
100 Bush Street (corner of Battery)
(415) 989-2233
Located on the second floor of the old Shell Building. Cafeteria style restaurant with a menu that changes daily. Reasonable.

Campton Place
340 Stockton Street
San Francisco (415) 781-5155.
Breakfast, weekend brunch, lunch and dinner. American cuisine. Very Expensive.

Green's
Building A Fort Mason
(415)-6222.
A California cuisine vegetarian menu with a variety of fresh organic produce. Expensive.

Zuni Cafe
1658 Market Street
(415) 552-2522.
European-style cafe. Large variety. Reasonable.

Chapter Eight

San Francisco Restaurants

Chinese Food

China Moon
639 Post Street
(415) 775-4789.
Small informal restaurant. Reasonable.

The Mandarin
Ghirardelli Square
(415) 673-8812.
Lunch and dinner. Expensive.

French

Masa's
648 Bush Street in the Vintage Court Hotel
This restaurant has received top reviews from top reviewers. Very Expensive.

Zola's
1722 Sacramento Street
(415) 775-3311.
Small bistro. Reasonable.

Indian

Gaylord India Restaurant
Ghirardelli Square
(415) 771-8822.
Dinner. Chain restaurant from Bombay.
Expensive.

Italian

Basta Pasta
1268 Grant Avenue in North Beach
(415) 434-2248.
Fettuccine and spaghetti with a variety of
sauces. Fresh fish. Reasonable.

Tommaso's
1042 Kearny Street in North Beach
(415) 398-9696
Pizza served here for more than fifty years.
Casual. Inexpensive. No reservations.

Japanese

Sanppo
1702 Post Street
(415) 346-3486.
Small casual restaurant. Very busy. Inexpensive.

Russian

George's Specialties
3420 Balboa Street
(415) 752-4009.
Beef stroganoff, chicken kiev. Expensive.

Thai

Khan Toke Thai House
5937 Geary
(415) 668-6654
One of the first Thai restaurants in San Francisco
Bay Area. Reasonable.

9

Chapter
Nine

Northern
California

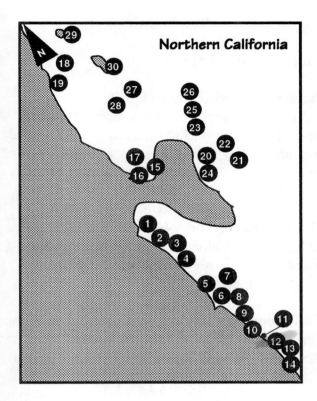

Northern California

1. Fitzgerald Marine Reserve
2. Pillar Point Harbor
3. Half Moon Bay
4. Pigeon Pt. Lighthouse
5. Ano Nuevo State Reserve
6. Santa Cruz/Lighthouse
7. Roaring Camp Railroad
8. Monterey
9. Cannery Row
10. Pacific Grove
11. Carmel
12. Point Lobos
13. Big Sur
14. Hearst Castle
15. Sausalito

16. Muir Woods
17. Mt. Tamalpais
18. Fort Bragg
19. Mendocino
20. Jack London Square
21. Lakeside Park
22. Oakland Zoo
23. Berkeley
24. Tilden Park
25. Behring Museum
26. Lindsay Museum
27. Napa
28. Sonoma
29. Clear Lake
30. Lake Berryessa

The Coastline

South of San Francisco

Fitzgerald Marine Reserve   This is one of California's largest natural tide pools. You can observe abalone, starfish, and many other marine creatures at low tide. Tours are available. Hwy 1 and California Avenue in Moss Beach. (415) 728-3584.

Pillar Point Harbor   Located just north of Half Moon Bay along Hwy 1. Whale watching cruises and deep sea fishing boat excursions. (415) 726-4382.

Half Moon Bay   Known as Spanishtown at one time and now calls itself the "Pumpkin Capital of the World". The Great Pumpkin Festival is held in October which includes a parade down Main Street and a pumpkin carving contest for children. Several Christmas tree farms are located in the area along with the Obester Winery which is about one mile east of Half Moon Bay right along Highway 92. (415) 726-5202.

Pigeon Point Lighthouse   Located along Highway 1 in Pescadero on Pigeion Point Road. Built in 1872. Tours are available (415) 879-0633.

Ano Nuevo State Reserve   This reserve is about twenty five miles south of Half Moon Bay and is the breeding ground for the elephant seal. Guided tours are offered December through April. (415) 879-0227.

Chapter Nine

The Coastline

Santa Cruz

Santa Cruz is a city by the sea with beautiful
white sand beaches, Victorian homes, seafood
restaurants and an oceanfront amusement park,
the Boardwalk. The Boardwalk includes several
concession stands, game booths and many rides
including the Giant Dipper wooden roller coaster.
The University of California at Santa Cruz is
located on a hillside of redwood trees. Santa Cruz
has been completely rebuilt and renovated since
he earthquake of 1989. On the municipal wharf
you can buy fresh seafood and don't miss the sea
lions under the pier, the surfing museum and the
Cocoanut Grove (a Victorian ballroom) and the
Sun Room restaurant.

**Chapter
Nine**

**Santa
Cruz**

Santa Cruz Big Trees and Pacific Railway

The Roaring Camp Railroad is located in Felton
on Graham Hill and Mt. Herman Roads off
Highway 17. You can also ride the "Suntan
Special" train to the Santa Cruz Beach and
Boardwalk. The return trip can have quite a wait,
especially if you spend the day at the beach and
wait for the late train back. (418) 335-4484.

Santa Cruz Lighthouse

Along West Cliff Drive stands this lighthouse
with a unique surfing museum housed inside. The
museum displays old surfboard photos and old
surfboards that have used on the Santa Cruz
beaches over the past one hundred years.
(408) 429-3429.

The Monterey Peninsula

The beauty of the Monterey Peninsula is unmatched anywhere else in California. Cypress trees hug the rocky coastline along with many championship oceanfront golf courses. The 17 Mile Drive in Pebble Beach takes you along the ocean towards Carmel through a forest of tall Monterey Cypress trees. Deer inhabit the golf courses inside the gates of this forest. Carmel is a quaint small town with many art galleries and not a single stop light. Pacific Grove is a picturesque oceanfront town of restored Victorian homes.

Chapter Nine

The Monterey Peninsula

Monterey   Monterey's Fisherman's Wharf is a great place to stroll and visit the many gift shops and outdoor fish markets. The marina is a beautiful view from any one of the seafood restaurants lining the wharf. **Dennis the Menace Park** is located nearby adjacent to Lake El Estero. This children's park is wonderful in that there is only one entrance and exit. The park has many imaginative attractions.

Pacific Grove   Monarch butterflies cover the tree's from late October to March on Ridge Road off of Lighthouse Avenue. Pacific Grove is nicknamed "Butterfly City USA". The Pacific Grove coastline is covered with a beautiful pathway rich in purple flowering iceplant. The rocky beaches and shoreline tidepools offer a spectacular view. The town is filled with Victorian designed homes and inns.

Cannery Row   Following to the south side
of Fisherman's Wharf in Monterey, is Cannery
Row. Once bustling with sardine canneries, this
row is now converted to an assortment of shops
and restaurants and the home of the **Monterey
Bay Aquarium.** This aquarium is one of the best
of its kind and is a must see while visiting the
peninsula. The exhibits include The Kelp Forest
exhibit which displays the underwater life in a
local kelp forest through the use of a giant 300
million gallon tank containing rays, sharks, kelp
and an assortment of Pacific Ocean fish life.
(408) 648-4888.

Carmel   Carmel is a village of more than
sixty five art galleries, many restaurants, specialty stores, and inns. There are no stop lights in
the village and the town is best travelled by foot.
In the summer you can stroll through Carmel via
the Carmel Art Walk. Refreshments are served at
some of the galleries. Carmel Beach is a beautiful
white sand beach with a sweeping view of Carmel
Bay and Pebble Beach. The surf is unsafe for
swimming. Local surfers can be seen riding the
waves at the south end of the beach.   The
Thunderbird Book Store located in The Barnyard
also has a small restaurant and a huge children's
section. You can read books while dining.

Point Lobos State Reserve

Sea otters and seals can be seen year round in this scenic reserve. Guided nature walks are available and a limited number of certified scuba divers may obtain diving permits by reservation to scuba dive in Whalers Cove (800) 444-7275. There are many hiking trails with more than six miles of hiking. The reserve is a spectacular blend of beaches, Monterey cypress trees and rocky coastline. 408-624-4909.

Big Sur

Just south of Point Lobos is the beautiful Big Sur coastline. Fishing, hiking, camping, nature walks and swimming are offered. Pfeiffer Big Sur and Andrew Molera offer campsites and picnic facilities. Garrapata State Park has coastal access. 408-667-2315.

Hearst Castle/San Simeon

There are four different tours available to see this one hundred twenty five acre estate. Tour one covers the gardens, the pools, the guest house and the first floor of the home. The fourth tour is the"behind the scenes tour". Evening tours are also available. Reservations may be made through the California State Parks System phone number 800-444-7275.

North Bay

Sausalito

Sausalito is in the setting of a seacoast village with many art galleries, specialty shops and restaurants. Located just north of San Francisco over the Golden Gate Bridge. There are plenty of galleries and shops in the Plaza Vina del Mar and multi level Village Fair both on Bridgeway. You can also visit the San Francisco Bay Model Visitors Center (415) 332-2871 and see a working hydrolic model of the bay operated by the United States Army Corps Engineers and located on the corner of Bridgeway and Spring Street.

Muir Woods

Named after John Muir, founder of the Sierra Club. There are more than twenty five miles of trails in this five hundred acre park. The road to Muir Woods is winding and narrow.   Camping and picknicking are not permitted.
(415) 388-2595.

Mt. Tamalpais State Park

From Muir Beach up to the top of the 2,500 foot Mt. Tamalpais are many hiking and riding trails.

Near the park headquarters are picnic areas and campsites. In May and June, stage plays are presented in an outdoor hillside amphitheater.
(415) 388-2070.

Chapter Nine

North Bay

Fort Bragg

The California Western Rail Road Skunk Train runs from Fort Bragg to Willets on a scenic 40 mile trip through redwood groves. Entering Fort Bragg, you cross over the Noyo River on a high bridge. Fort Bragg is the largest town along the coast and was once an army post and a lumber town. 707-964-6371.

Mendocino

Mendocino is located along the rugged coastline north of Point Arena. The houses in the village of Mendocino reflect a New England Cape Cod architecture. The village has many art galleries, restaurants and specialty shops. The local Art Center hosts many performing art productions. There are many bed and breakfast inns in Mendocino. Some of the farmland in this area has recently been developed by wine growers.

Redwood Tree Parks

Along the northernmost coastline of California are several redwood tree parks where you can see some of the tallest redwood trees in the world. Some of the trees reach over three hundred fifty feet in height. The Redwood National Park covers more than one hundred thousand acres including large redwood groves. Also are the Del Norte Coast Redwoods State Park, Jedediah Smith Redwoods State Park, Humboldt Lagoons State Park and Humboldt Redwoods State Park.

East Bay

Oakland

Jack London Square Jack London Square is at the end of Broadway overlooking the Oakland Estuary. Jack London Village is a 1900's shopping complex with many seafood restaurants and shops. (510) 893-7956.

Lakeside Park Lakeside Park is on the east shore of Lake Merrit and includes a Children's Faryland which is said to be the inspiration for Disneyland. Lake Merrit is a natural salt water lake. A Garden Center and Natural Science Center are also located here. (510) 452-2259.

Oakland Zoo The Oakland Zoo is located in Knowland Park off of Hwy 580. Although this zoo is small it offers a nice Baby Zoo where children can pet and feed small animals. (510) 632-9523.

Berkeley

UC Berkeley is north of Oakland between Hearst and Bancroft (510) 652-5215.The campus art museum includes work by Rubens, Mark Rokthko and Cezanne. The Lawrence Hall of Science on Centennial Drive (510) 642-5132 and the Lowie Museum of Anthropology in Kroeber Hall on College and Bancroft (510) 642-3681 are interesteing places to visit. Telegraph Avenue offers many bookstore/coffeeshops.

Chapter Nine

East Bay

135

Charles Lee Tilden Regional Park Take Marin Street and follow the signs to the 2,065 acre park containing a minifarm, golfcourse, lakes picnic areas, hiking tennis, etc. (510) 5331-9300. Grizzly Peak Blvd. also takes you up to a 1,600-foot lookout.

Behring Auto Museum

This museum displays more than one hundred rare automobiles, some worth more than one million dollars. The collection includes Johnny Rutherford's Indianapolis 500 winning race car. The second floor of the museum has rotating exhibits. Located in Danville on Blackhawk Plaza Circle. (510) 736-2277.

Lindsay Museum

Located in Walnut Creek on First Avenue. This newly built museum has a collection of native live animals, some of which children may pet. The museum is well known for its Wildlife Rehabilitation Program. Classes are offered. (510) 935-1978.

Wine Country

The Napa-Sonoma region of northern California is generally referred to as wine country. Some vineyards in this region date back to 1780. Mendocino, Lake and Monterey counties are known as newly emerging wine regions. In general, California produces about ninety percent of America's grape harvest, with most of the grapes being crushed into wine. The most popular time to visit the Napa-Sonoma region is in the fall when the grapes are harvested.

Napa

Napa is located at the south end of the Napa Valley which is the best known wine region in the United States. Between Napa and Calistoga, along route 29 are as many as two hundred wineries and more than 22,000 acres of vineyards.

The town of Napa is refurbished and graced with many shops, restaurants and inns with Victorian design. Contact the Napa Valley Visitors Bureau for more information   (707) 226-7459. Event hotline (707) 963-1112. Other wineries and historic sites can be found in the Napa Valley towns of Yountville, Oakville, Rutherford, St. Helena, and Calistoga. The Robert Mondavi Winery in Oakville offers advance reservation tours. Charles Krug, Christian Brothers ,Beringer, Sutter Home and Louis Martini wineries all are located within the area of St. Helena. Specialty shopping for fine foods and wines and dining is especially enjoyable in these quaint towns.

Chapter Nine

Wine Country

Sonoma

Sonoma County is west of Napa County and east of the Pacific Ocean. The town of Sonoma is about an hour north of San Francisco. Sonoma Plaza is in the center of town which was once the location of a revolution when over one hundred and fifty years ago the settlers defied the Mexican rule until the United States government intervened and California became a new state. The plaza is filled with many fine dining spots, specialty shops and galleries.

Clear Lake

Clear Lake just three hours from Palo Alto and just north of Calistoga. The area offers expensive resort lodging, private tennis and golf facilities as well as campsites and cabin lodging. Clear Lake is California's largest natural lake and is known for great bass fishing. The lake also offers sailing, boating and water skiing. (707) 994-3600.

Lake Berryessa

This lake is popular for fishing, boating and water skiing. Located west of the Napa Valley. On the west side of the lake are motels and campsites. For boat launching information, you can call the Lake Berryessa phone number: (707) 966-2111.

10

Chapter Ten

Child Care and Schools

Child Care Information

Office of Child and Family Services

This service provides a variety of options for childcare services to Stanford families. This office assists families in finding quality child care arrangements in university child care homes, preschools or child care centers in the Stanford area. The family home care is provided by spouses of Stanford graduate students primarily serving infants and toddlers up to the age of three. For a brochure and more information, please call (415) 723-2660.

Children's Center of the Stanford Community

695 Pampas Lane, Stanford, CA 94305 (415) 853-3090. CCSC is a parent-cooperative child care center that has been operating since 1971 as an independent nonprofit corporation. Parent participation is required. Full and part time care is available.

Stanford Arboretum Children's Center

211 Quarry Road, Stanford, CA 94305 (415) 725-6322. This program began in 1988 and is operated as a nonprofit corporation. Enrollment is limited to affiliates of Stanford University, Stanford Hospital, and the Lucile Packard Children's Hospital at Stanford. This program features flexible scheduling for families with several options for full or part time care.

140

Child Care Scholarships

A number of years ago the Dorothea K. Almond Scholarship Fund was established to provide child care subsidies to families. The funds are distributed on a greatest needs basis. Applications are available in the Office of Child & Family Services. Campus programas vary in costs depending on the age of the child and the type of program. The fees are typically increased five to ten per cent each year.

Community Coordinated Child Development Council; (4C's of Santa Clara County)

160 E. Virginia Street, San Jose, 95112 (408) 0900. This is a non-profit organization providing child care referrals. Information is available on licensed centers and licensed family child care homes.

Palo Alto Community Child Care

3990 Ventura Street, Palo Alto, 94306 (415) 493-2361. PACC has sixteen centers in Palo Alto providing care for infants, toddlers, preschool aged and school based extended care. The city of Palo Alto sponsors this program.

Child Care Resource and Referral Center

Stanford Administration Building
859 Escondido Road
Stanford CA 94305 (415) 723-2660.

141

Preschool Information

Bing School, Stanford University
850 Escondido Road, Stanford, CA 94305
(415) 723-4865. Bing School offers several
programs for both toddlers and preschoolers.
Openings are filled to Stanford affiliated families
ahead of newcomers not affiliated with Stanford.

**Chapter
Ten**

**Preschool
Information**

Escondido Children's Center
845 Escondido Road, Stanford
(415) 723-0217. Escondido Nursery School is a
parent cooperative preschool located in the
Escondido Children's Center. This school primarily serves Escondido Village resideints and other
Stanford affiliates.

Parents' Nursery School Co-op
2328 Louis Road, Palo Alto, CA
(415) 856-1440. Parent's Nursery School is a
parent cooperative in which the parents volunteer
and participate in the program one morning per
week. Parents' has an endowed scholarship fund
especially for Stanford families. Last minute
openings are saved every year for newcoming
Stanford families.

Palo Alto Unified School District
Pre-School Family & Young Fives
4120 Middlefield Road
Palo Alto
(415) 856-0833

Pre-School Family

The Pre-School Family Program is offerred by the Palo Alto Unified School District Department of Adult Education. More than fifteen classes are offerred from a Newborn Class to a Four Year Old Program. There are participation classes and observation classes. Spring pre-registration is recommended . All classes meet at Greendell School, 4120 Middlefield Road, Palo Alto, 94303.

Young Fives

Young Fives is a special program offered by the Palo Alto Unified Schools for children whose parents feel their child is not ready to enter kindergarten. Young Fives is not intended to replace kindergarten. It is intended as an extra year before kindergarten.

Parents participate in the program one day each week. Parents also attend two adult discussion meetings per month at night from 7:30p.m. to 10:00p.m. Must be a Palo Alto resident to qualify (includes Stanford).

School Districts

**Chapter
Ten**

**School
Districts**

Palo Alto Unified School District
25 Churchill Avenue
Palo Alto, 94306

Los Altos Elementary School District
1299 Bryant Avenue
Mountain View, 940-4650

Mountain View Elementary School District
District Office
220 View
Mountain View, 968-6565

Menlo Park City School District
Administration-Superintendent
181 Encinal Avenue
Atherton, 321-7140

It is best to register your child(ren) for school as soon as you receive your letter of acceptance. To register your child you will need a birth certificate or passport, proof of where you will be living, and a record of immunizations dated and signed by a physician or health care provider.

Appendix

Libraries

Palo Alto Libraries   The libraries offer many services such as rental art, free videos, children's story hours, and special children's events. The summer brings the summer reading program which includes "Wacky Wednesdays", a super program that brings many special talents to the different libraries for very special activities related to children and reading.   Check the library closest to you for more information.

Main Library, 1213 Newell Road
(near Embarcadero) 329-2436

Children's Library, 1276 Harriet, 329-2134
Storytimes: (18 months - 3 years) Fridays
10:30a.m. Preschool (3 - 5 years) Fourth
Saturday of each month 10:30 a.m.

College Terrace, 2300 Wellesley, 329-2298
Storytime: (18 months - 3 years)   Wednesdays
10:30a.m.

Mitchell Park, 3700 Middlefield, 329-2586
Storytime: (18 months - 3 years)   Tuesdays
10:30 a.m.

Downtown, 270 Forest Ave., 329-2641
Terman Park, 661 Arastradero, 329-2606

Mountain View Library

585 Franklin (415) 903-6887
Children's Services (415) 903-6888
Please call for storytime registration information.
Storytimes: All storytimes are at 10:30 a.m.
Tuesdays: 4 year old- Reading Readiness
Wednesdays: 3 year olds- Stories Plus
Thursdays: 2 year olds- Toddlers
Saturdays: All ages.

Menlo Park Library

This library has been recently renovated and offers a wonderful children's section. Many activities to choose from during the year.
800 Alma Menlo Park (415) 858-3460
Children's Section (415) 858-3464.

Storytimes:
Wednesdays at 10:00a.m. or 11:00a.m. Toddlers
Wednesdays at 7:00 p.m. All Ages
Pajamas Storytime
Thursdays: 10:30 a.m. Preschoolers

Portola Valley Library

Located right next to an art museum on Portola Valley road. Watch for special programs. 765 Portola Valley Road. 851-0560.

Post Offices

Palo Alto Main Post Office
380 Hamilton Avenue 323-1321

Stanford University Branch
(next to Stanford Book Store) 322-0059

Town and Country Village Substation
Town and Country Pharmacy
On Embarcadero and El Camino
Does not offer complete services of regular
post offices. Stamps available.

Cambridge Station
265 Cambridge Avenue
(415) 327-4174

Mountain View Main Post Office
211 Hope
Mountain View, (415) 967-5721

Menlo Park Main Post Office
3875 Bohannon Drive
Menlo Park, (415) 323-0038

Department of Motor Vehicles

California has smog requirements for all vehicles.
As you may be new to California, you will need to
check with the local DMV to see about obtaining
the required smog certificate. Many service
stations issue these certificates. The DMV can
also provide you with a study booklet for taking
your driver's license exam. To register your car

and obtain a California Driver's License, make an appointment with the DMV. The process can be confusing and time consuming. AAA of California offers car registration appointments for members.

DMV Mountain View Office
595 Showers Drive
Mountain View, (415) 968-0610

DMV Redwood City Office
300 Brewster Avenue
Redwood City, (415) 368-2837

Department of Parks and Recreation
P.O. Box 2390
Sacramento, CA 95811
(916) 445-6477
You can make camping reservations by phone, mail or in person up to eight weeks in advance or as late as two days before your trip. (800) 444-7275.

California Office of Tourism
1121 L Street
Suite 103
Sacramento, 95814
(916) 322-1396

National Forest Information
California Region
U.S. Forest Service
630 Sansome Street
San Francisco, CA 94111
(415) 556-0122

Airports

San Francisco International Airport   Located off of highway 101 along the San Francisco Bay waterfront between San Bruno and Millbrae. (415) 876-7809. Many commercial airlines have terminals at this airport including both domestic and international flights. United Airlines has a larger terminal at SFO.

San Jose International Airport   Serviced by more than ten different airlines offering domestic and international flights. American Airlines has a large terminal at this airport. Located off of highway 101 in San Jose. (408) 277-4759.

Transportation

Amtrak train service is available throughout California offering train routes from Seattle, Washington to San Diego, California. For reservations and schedule information (800) 872-7245.

Cal Train offers train service from San Francisco to San Jose. There are twenty five station stops in between. The train runs often. For fare and schedule information call (800) 660-4287.

Sam Trans offers bus service in San Mateo County and provides service to San Francisco and to the San Francisco International Airport. (800) 660-4287.

Santa Clara County Transit offers bus service with more than seventy five routes extending from Menlo Park to Los Gatos. (408) 321-2300 for route information. Exact change is required.

Greyhound For information on Greyhound bus services you can call (415) 558-6789 in San Francisco. (415) 961-3422 in Mountain View and (408) 297-8890 in San Jose

BART runs from Fremont to Richmond and from Concord to Daly City. For fare and schedule information, call (415) 793-BART.

Bicycle Groups

Western Wheelers Bicycle Club, Inc.
P.O. Box 518
Palo Alto, CA 94302

Sierra Club Bicycle Group
3632 Lawton #5
San Francisco, CA 94122
(415) 665-7913

Silicon Valley Bicycle Coalition
PO Box 831
Cupertino, CA 95015-0831
(415) 965-8456

San Francisco Bicycle Coalition
PO Box 22554
San Francisco, CA 94122
(415) 750-7075.

Bike Shops

Chain Reaction Bicycles
1451 El CAmino Real
Redwood City. (415) 366-7130.

Pacific Bicycle
1040 Grant Road
Mountain View (415) 961-9142.

Newspapers

San Francisco Chronicle
925 Mission Street, San Francisco, CA 94119.
The Chronicle is a major San Francisco newspaper with a large Sunday edition. 800-281-2476

The San Francisco Examiner
925 Mission Street, San Francisco, CA 94119.
The Examiner is similar to the Chronicle.
800-954-7777.

San Jose Mercury News
750 Ridder Park Driver, San Jose, CA 95131
The Mercury News is the large paper serving the
South Bay area. (415) 494-3188.

Palo Alto Weekly
703 High Street, Palo Alto, CA 94301.
A local newspaper with a mid week and weekend
edition. (415) 326-8210.

The Stanford Daily
Storke Student Publications Building, Stanford,
CA 94305. (415) 723-2554.

The Campus Report
Press Courtyard, Santa Teresa Street, Stanford, CA 94305. (415) 723-2558.

Mid-Peninsula Citizens for Fair Housing
457 Kingsley Avenue
Palo Alto, CA 94301 (415) 327-1718.
This office offers assistance in discrimination complaints.

Landlord Tenant Mediation Task Force
3390 Ventura Court, Room 9
Palo Alto, CA 94306. (415) 856-4062.

Utilities

Pacific Bell (415) 645-8643
Pacific Gas and Electric (415) 280-1212

Palo Alto Utilities (415) 329-2161

California Water Service (415) 968-1686
(Mountain View, Sunnyvale and Cupertino)
California Water Service (415) 367-6800
(Menlo Park, Portola Valley, Woodside)
Palo Alto Water Service(415) 329-2161
Redwood City Water Service (415) 780-7210
Mountain View Water Service (415) 966-6329
San Jose Water Company (408)279-7900
North San Jose Water Service (408) 277-4036
Santa Clara Water Service (408) 984-5111
Sunnyvale Water Service (408) 730-7400

Disposal Services

Each of the listed disposal companies below
offers a curbside recycling program such that you
can leave on the curb in specially marked bins;
newspapers, glass, and aluminum. Free recycling bins are provided.

Browning-Ferris Industries (415) 592-2411
(Menlo Park, East Palo Alto)
Foothill Disposal Company (415) 967-3034
(Mountain View)
Green Valley Disposal (408) 354-2100
(Los Gatos, Campbell)
Los Altos Garbage Company (415) 961-8040
(Cupertino, Los Altos Hills, Los Altos,
Portola Valley)
Palo Alto Sanitation Company (415) 493-4894
Peninsula Sanitary Service (415) 321-4236
(Stanford)

Recreation Departments

Cupertino	(408) 865-1384
Los Altos	(415) 941-0950
Los Gatos	(408) 358-3741
Menlo Park	(415) 858-3472
Mountain View	(415) 903-6331
Palo Alto	(415) 329-2261
San Jose	(408) 277-4661
Santa Clara	(408) 984-3223
Sunnyvale	(408) 730-7350

Resources

Books /Bibliography

Bargain Hunting in the Bay Area
by Sally Socolich. Wingbow Press, c1990.
This book covers outlet stores, secondhand trade
stores, thrift shops and general bargain shopping
in the San Francisco Bay Area.

**Bay Play, Complete Guide to the Best
Children's Activities in the Bay Area** by Susan
Andrews. Conari Press, c 1989.
Very resourceful book including day camp and
sports camp directories.

California State Parks by John Robinson, Sunset
Books, Lane Books, c 1972. A great book for
elaborate descriptions about the many beautiful
state parks in the Bay Area and along the Pacific
Coast.

Child Care Directory of Santa Clara County
by Community Coordinated Child Development
Council of Santa Clara County, c 1986. A great
resource book for learning more about child care
options in Santa Clara County.

Family Bike Rides by Milton A. Grossberg.
Chronicle Books, c1981. Information where to
go with the family for an afternoon bikeride.
Includes Alameda, San Mateo, and Santa Clara
counties.

Kidding Around San Francisco by Rosemary Zibart. John Muir Publications, c1989. This book is written for the child to read aged 8 and up. Information provided includes maps and child-oriented descriptions of events and places in San Francisco.

Places to Go with Children in Nothern California by Elizabeth Pomada. Chronicle Books, c1989. This book offers information on family recreation in Northern California.

Playgrounds of the Peninsula by Ava Zelver Everett. Tioga Publishing Company, c 1988. This book offers a thoughtful family-oreinted description of 74 public parks.

San Francisco Family Fun by Carole Tellingwinger Meyers. Carousel Press, c 1990. Offers information on restaurants, taverns, hotels, museums, parks, and plenty of things to do in San Francisco.

San Francisco Insider's Guide by John Bailey. Non-stop Books, c1980. This book offers a different look at where to go. Does offer information on restaurants, best bets and the outdoors.

San Francisco on a Shoestring by Louis Madison. A.M. Simmermann, c1989. From bed & breakfast to apartments and hotels with kitchens, this book offers information on budget living in San Francisco.

An Outdoor Guide to the San Francisco Bay Area by Dorothy L. Whitnah, Wilderness Press, c 1989. A guide for hiking, backpacking, biking and more in Marin, Napa, Sonoma, Alameda and Contra Costa counties as well as San Francisco and the peninsula.

The Complete Guide to the Golden Gate National Recreation Area by Karen Liberatore, Goodchild Jacobsen, c 1982. Very thorough book describing the GGNRA complete with interesting historical facts and comments.

Peninsula Trails by Jean Rusmore and Frances Spangl, Wilderness Press, c 1989. Includes hiking trails from San Francisco to Saratoga along with descriptive trail notes and maps.

Adventuring in the San Francisco Bay Area by Peggy Wayburn, Sierra Club Books, 1987. This book offers information on oudoor reacreational activites in the nine major Bay Area counties.

SJ's Winners, An Exceptional Approach to Round-the -World Wining and Dining in the San Francisco Bay Area by Serena Jutkovitz, Russian Hill House Books, c 1982. A descriptive book about where,when, how to dine in the Bay Area.

Restaurants of San Francisco by Patricia Unterman and Stan Sesser, Chronicle Books, c 1988. Two well qualified restaurant critics rate more than one hundred San Francisco restaurants.

Best Restaurants San Francisco & Northern California Jacqueline Killeen, Charles Miller, Critic Publishing Company, c 1980. Reviews more than 100 restaraunts from Reno, Nevada to the Monterey Penninsula.

San Francisco and Beyond, 101 Free or Affordable Excursions by Pamela P. Hegarty, Travel for Less Press, c 1992. Amusements, landmarks, towns, outdoor adventures all described in a simple to read fashion.

Guide to the Good Life at Stanford , Good Life Publications, c 1991. Many dining, entertainment, shopping, and recreation spots listed and described. Also covers Marin and Berkely.

Bay Area Bike Rides by Ray Hosler, Chronicle Books, c 1990. Written by a San Francisco Chronicle cycling columnist.Very organized book with maps and mileage markers. Easy to understand.

South Bay Trails by Frances Spangle and Jean Rusmore, Wilderness Press, c 1991. Describes many of the trails in the Santa Clara Valley along with trail notes and pictures.

The Bay Area at Your Feet by Margot Doss, Don't Call it Frisco Press, c 1988. Written by a columnist for the San Francisco Chronicle who describes walks in the seven counties surrounding the San Francisco Bay.

Sunset Travel Guide to Northern California by Editors of Sunset, Lane Books, c 1980. Describes San Francisco, the surrounding Bay Area, the Monterey Peninsula and more of Northern California. Listings helpful for campsites, skiing etc.

Discover the Californias, California Tourism Corporation, c 1992. An official California Travel Guide free by calling (800) 862-2543.

California State Parks by Kim Heacox, Falcon Press Publishing, c 1987. A very colorful book with many beautiful color photos accompanied by text rich in California history.

Making the Most of Sonoma County by Don Edwards, Valley of the Moon Press, c 1986. Described in detail where to visit in all of Sonoma County from Santa Rosa to the coast. Visitors services listed in the back.

Touring San Francisco Bay Area by Bicycle by Peter Powers, Terragraphics, c 1990. Amazing computer generated graphics in this pocket sized travel book, plus special footnotes about local bicyclists who happen to own local bike stores.

Index

M

167

169

To Order Additional Copies
of this Book:

Send Postal Orders to:

Napa Sonoma Press
P.O. Box 1133
Palo Alto, CA 94301
(415) 322-6556

Sales Tax:

California residents, please add 8.25% sales tax

Shipping:

Book Rate: $1.00 for the first book and .50 for
each additional book.
First Class: $2.00 per book

Payment:

Please include check or money order payable to:
Napa Sonoma Press

Name: _____

Street: _____

City: _____

State: _____ **Zip:** _____

	Price:	9.95
(In CA only)	**Tax:**	
	Shipping:	
	Total:	

Satisfaction Guaranteed

If for any reason you are not satisfied, you may return
your book and your full purchase price will be refunded.

To Order Additional Copies
of this Book:

Send Postal Orders to:

Napa Sonoma Press
P.O. Box 1133
Palo Alto, CA 94301
(415) 322-6556

Sales Tax:

California residents, please add 8.25% sales tax

Shipping:

Book Rate: $1.00 for the first book and .50 for
each additional book.
First Class: $2.00 per book

Payment:

Please include check or money order payable to:
Napa Sonoma Press

Name: _____

Street: _____

City: _____

State: _____ **Zip:** _____

Price:	9.95	
(In CA only) **Tax:**		
Shipping:		
Total:		

Satisfaction Guaranteed
If for any reason you are not satisfied, you may return
your book and your full purchase price will be refunded.